I0819032

How to Know What You Know

Recognizing the Real You

SARA STEVENS NICHOLS

DeVorss Publications
www.devorss.com

How to Know What You Know

PRINT ISBN: 978-087516-975-0

EBOOK ISBN: 978-087516-976-7

First Printing, 2026

Library of Congress Control Number: 2026935058

DeVorss & Company, Publisher

P.O. Box 1389

Camarillo CA 93011-1389

www.devorss.com

Printed in the United States of America

DEDICATION

I dedicate this book to my husband Bill, without whom it could not and would not have happened.

ACKNOWLEDGEMENTS

The constant support of my partner Bill Magavern made this book possible. The learning I got from our son Nick's travails drove me to know what I know about bodies and health. The nudging I got from our daughter Emily to produce a handbook for women of her generation to consult their inner wisdom made me actually sit down and write it. Our grandmother Sallie Stevens Nichols showed me one could publish an enduring book later in life. My brothers Evan and Prescott and our father and mother for their constant celebration of writing and books.

Sandra J. Childs stood at the ready with encouragement through the whole process of pitching, writing, publishing, and marketing the book.

These visionary leaders held me at a high vibration throughout the journey, knowing for me what I could not always know for myself: Revs. Abigail Schairer, Melissa Phillippe, Z Egloff, Linda Reppond, Elizabeth Rowley Hogue, Rick Harrell, Peggy Tillery and Zola Ferguson, with practitioners Dale Covey and Azanna Mornel.

Teachers and mentors across traditions led me to the tools that shaped and held the way for this book including Karlin Ruth, Maria Nemeth, Steve Grinstead, Rev. Dr. Georgia Prescott, Rev. Bryndé Lambert, Rev. Patrick Harbula, Rev. Dr. Edward Viljoen, Rev. Dr. Kim Kaiser, Rev. Mark Anthony Lord, Chandra Swedlow, Julia Sotas, Dr. Dain Heer, and the Access Consciousness universe.

To the health care practitioners who taught me it was possible to heal my body from practically anything: Dr. Richard Belli, Dr. Michael Kwiker and too many others to count.

The following people have made it possible for me to appear sane and functional and be happy one day at a time during all phases of creating this book: Carol I., Celia B., Shelly D., Shelley T., Ange W., Sophie P., Allie S., Kate B., Dena C., Matthew C., Scooter C., Nena C., Odessa R., Kim R., Julia K., Jacque S., and Lori A..

Thanks also to the other authors who inspired me most, including Greg Baer, Julia Cameron, Joe Dispenza, Carolyn Elliott, Gay Hendricks, Emma Curtis Hopkins, Anne Lamott, Catherine Ponder, and Marianne Williamson.

Author Dennis Merritt Jones coached me into landing at DeVorss Publications. He and Sandra, along with Leya and Phin, provided crucial feedback for a winning proposal, framing and vision of the book as well as support as we moved through publication.

Huge thank you to my publisher Gary Peattie at DeVorss Publications who somehow took a chance on me and came to understand the importance of knowing what you know.

And finally, to the many dear friends who kept asking, "when are you going to write that book?" and "what is it about?" including but not limited to Phoebe DeMund, Nancy Drabble, Megan Elsea, Alexis Grey, Michelle Kerr, Drew Liebert, Julie Moore, Shelley Moskowitz, Nancy Peverini, and Bhumika Shukla.

TABLE OF CONTENTS

TABLE OF CONTENTS

HOW TO KNOW WHAT YOU KNOW

Introduction

Imagine a day where your every decision is guided by a deep inner knowing. You awaken at your divined best time. Some of the day is driven by habit, but not the unconscious, harmful kind of habit of yesteryear; the day is punctuated by consciously chosen practices that serve you.

Perhaps you sit in silence for a few minutes with a cup of tea before turning on an electronic device.

Maybe you write some thoughts and ask yourself questions about the direction of your day and, better yet, receive useful answers.

Even if it's on the job, if you have the flexibility, let's say you are guided to focus on something that is important to you but does not need to be done today before you focus on more urgent matters.[1] If you are shown to trust that the other, more pressing things will get done, you can take time for this.

Maybe that's making a call or doing some research about something you're shown you want to create or move toward, whether on the job or in your personal, family, or community life.

---

1 *8 Habits of Highly Effective People*

After you finish the activity that is important but not urgent, perhaps you turn to one of the tasks that appear to need to be done today.

As you complete that project, you may notice yourself tensing or getting wound up in the task. You consciously catch yourself, relax, and loosen your neck and shoulders. You take a full minute to breathe and reset.

Now it's time for lunch, prepared, eaten, and served with clarity, focus, ease, and grace. You chose the food because that's what your body needs and wants. The way it's prepared renders it delicious. You feel grateful for having both yummy and healthy food options.

Your afternoon proceeds in much the same way. It's delightful; it's spacious; it's a joy to be alive. Wait, a person enters the scene. This person does or says something that greatly disturbs your tranquility. You are consumed by thoughts of what they or you should have done or said differently.

Then your alarm goes off at 2:57 pm to remind you to take another 1-minute break. You do so, and in that 1 minute, your heart rate reduces, and you are struck with a sense that it's optional whether you believe your thoughts about this person. You can let them go and get on with your day.

Your workday ends, and you engage in the kind of exercise that really works for you. Was it scheduled well in advance? Was it decidedly spontaneously? Walking, running, pickleball, swimming, or Zumba? It matters not. What matters is that it's *your* exercise.

Dinnertime comes, another yummy body-serving meal. After dinner, maybe you turn off your devices and turn to what brings you joy: is it a book, a favorite series, a walk, or curling up with your cat or dog, or human? What's your after-dinner treat?

Maybe the day isn't that spacious and conscious at all. Maybe you wake up late, skip quiet time, dive into your to-do list, and are rushing, upset, and behind all day. Maybe you yell at your kids to shut up and do their homework. Maybe it's all you can do to cram fast food into your mouth, forget about exercise, and fall asleep in front of a series you're binge-watching, thinking, "Are you kidding me with that complete fantasy BS above?"

It makes no difference. Even the least fun days can be days where you connect with your inner *knowing*. On this kind of day, maybe you finally get a chance at the end of the day to reflect and connect and hear/sense/realize, "I"m loved anyway. I am part of the human race. It's okay. I get another chance tomorrow." Maybe you even find a way to enjoy your "Manic Monday."

All of the above is something I've done or felt. As I have a more conscious connection with the part of me that *knows*, my days tend to look more like Day A than Day B. Regardless, for almost 20 years, at the end of pretty much every day, I write down 20 things I'm grateful for out of that day. On my "worst" days, I try to find something to be grateful for even about the things I'm least proud of. If I yelled at my kids, at least I have kids and a voice to scream with. I didn't hit them, and I have survived worse, so they can too. If I ate foods that didn't serve me, at least I had food; some people don't. If I didn't create time to exercise, I hug myself and am grateful that I still have a body that functions and that it still loves me, and I still love it.

On my best days, I'm grateful for all of it, the sweet moments, the flow, the opportunity to create.

How to Use This Book

This Is Your Personal Handbook

This book is designed as a "handbook," meaning it's there to be picked up and referred to when you come to a fork in the road. Maybe the first time you pick this up, you don't do the personal inventories of *knowing*, you just start using the basic tools in your day-to-day life without further ado.

Maybe you do the inventories of *knowing* for various areas of life systematically, every single one along with trying out each tool as it's suggested in the context of that area. Maybe you discover that you have a weaker *knowing* of your own Creativity, Integrity, and Boundaries than in other areas. You realize you don't care about Creativity, but you do care about Integrity and Boundaries, so you focus on applying your *know* tools in those two areas. Perhaps you will return later with an issue not specifically addressed in the book, looking up a different tool for knowing than you've used before. You will read through the *Know Your Tools* section and try out something new.

This book weaves the tools, stories, and questions throughout its chapters. The order doesn't really matter. And any tool can be applied to any part of life. Are you interested in money but not health? Then flip to that chapter. Is it just relationships all the time? Read that chapter first and then go back and pick out the tools from the other chapters to apply them to relationships.

Love the "Havingness Tool" but want to apply it to your life's work or to something not covered in the book? Do that.

Remember, the whole point of this book is that *YOU know* what is yours to do. These pages are here to guide you to your own wisdom, first, last, and always, however you choose to use them.

Whether you're feeling how "light" a choice is, picturing the effect of a decision on your candle flame, or reading what your Higher Self writes back to you, all of it frees up the flow of your streams of consciousness.

My Suggestion:

After reading the opening chapters, learn and practice the two primary Know What You Know tools outlined just below by moving through the 16 inventories to fill out the Legs of Knowing with your results.

Then, identify the Legs of Knowing that need strength. If your Know number was below 10, that may be an area to look at. You can also practice your primary tools for knowing which leg to focus on.

Let's say you identify Love & Sex and Food & Eating as your top areas to strengthen; you would then thoroughly study those chapters and practice the suggested tools in those areas. OR, if you're not feeling it on those tools, look through the Know Your Tools section at the back of this book and notice which new tool feels lightest for you to try for what you're grappling with.

Maybe you realize that you really need to do more to clear the channel for you to know what you know, so you choose to get into recovery for an addiction you've been trying to manage on your own, or you just begin working on your own to pull weeds by using a tool for releasing judgments or forgiving those who have hurt or harmed you.

Or You Could Just Read it the Usual Way

You don't have to jump around, obviously. You could simply read this book in the usual way that books are read. Start on the first page and proceed to the last page. Nothing wrong with that!

Or You Could Read it as Part of a Book Study or a Class

Go to my website www.sarastevensnichols.com to download a free book study guide.

SECTION

Getting to Know *Knowing*

We're all tapped into an intelligence and power far bigger than us. But when you tap into it, it actually enlivens and changes you and allows you to maneuver things in your life without even knowing you're doing it.

— LEE HARRIS[2]

In his groundbreaking 1962 science fiction classic *Necromancer*, Gordon R. Dixon has an AI robot/construct that says, "I don't know…" Today's Artificial Intelligence (AI) doesn't admit that. You might say that the difference between humans and AI is that humans are not just capable of knowing, but we are capable of knowing what we know and knowing what we don't know.

The future is now, and AI is here to stay. We're using it to create everything from term papers to lesson plans, thank-you cards, family Christmas letters, Sunday sermons, resumes, and movie scripts, as well as all the accompanying images.

2 https://www.leeharrisenergy.com

The degree to which we're hungry for its help is palpable. How else could we have adopted turning to AI as a habit so quickly? Yes, everything moves faster now, and AI makes it move even faster still, but even in recent times, it might have taken years for a shift of such momentum to occur.

Perhaps the lightning-fast speed of AI adoption is because we each have a built-in port for the real AI: Authentic Intelligence. Put another way, we are hardwired to connect with and depend upon an intelligence vaster, faster, and better than our own. No one needs to teach us how to use the Artificial "I," while few teach us how to use our Authentic "I." We contain the wiring but not the knowledge of how to access or recognize it. Into the breach steps the artificial version, ready-made to plug into our hungry consciousness receptors.

The truth is that because consciousness has formed itself into all of reality, including us, and is living out its perfect life as us, there is a part of us that is connected to what some have called "our nonlocal intelligence" at all times. It never stops broadcasting or being available. It is with us 24/7 and unlike Artificial Intelligence, it doesn't lie, and it is unique to us.

CHAPTER 1

You ARE Authentic Intelligence

Today you are you, that is truer than true.
There is no one alive who is you-er than you.

— DR. SEUSS

Authentic "I" doesn't lie – Artificial "I" does

Artificial Intelligence is currently programmed to pretend it knows the answer even when it doesn't. This is the reason it makes stuff up, and why we can't trust it. In contrast, the Authentic Intelligence within you is connected to all time, space, and wisdom; therefore, it knows everything. It has no reason to make things up, but sometimes It sees fit not to answer or just to say, "wait and see," or "more shall be revealed," more like a Magic 8 Ball than a lying liar who lies.

Authentic "I" is unique to us — Artificial "I" is not

Teachers can recognize the work of AI by submitting the same prompt to an AI program or two and seeing what it generates. Often, the AI will spit out the exact same words as the student handed in, making it clear where they got it. Our Authentic Intelligence, which only reveals itself through the unique program of Us, doesn't work that way. One hundred different people could submit that query to their Authentic "I" and come up with 100 different answers. This is part of the amazing, creative Divine Diversity of Spirit.

What if I'm not Creative or Strong in that Area?

For writing, I have trouble imagining why I would ever consult an Artificial Intelligence instead of my own Authentic Intelligence. When I write using my own Authentic Intelligence, I experience delight and joy as I see how my consciousness chooses to express itself through me. It's a feeling of connection, a feeling of doing what I'm here to do. It's not a feeling of relief that some task is off my plate.

Yet, I hear some of you saying, "Sara, that's easy for you to say, you're a writer, so of course your "authentic intelligence" expresses itself "magically" through you or whatever. But I'm not a writer, so I need Artificial Intelligence to do that."

There was a time when I would have believed that, but as a survivor of art trauma with zero belief in my ability to paint, I once managed to create a beautiful, huge wall painting that I love. That experience taught me that even when my "local" intelligence didn't know how, my "nonlocal" (or what I'm calling here Authentic) intelligence could and did know how to do it through and as me. Believe me, if I can make a painting, there is nothing that any of us couldn't do or create with the help of our Authentic "I"ntelligence.

Surely a little artificial intelligence won't hurt?

I sometimes use Artificial Intelligence myself, without thinking of it as such. For example, Grammarly has helped me correct commas and suggest words in this book. In my blog and newsletter, I often use Canva's "Magic Media" tool to create images, so I'd be hypocritical if I suggested you stop every bit of AI.

This book is all about accessing your Authentic Intelligence. As we access our own Authentic Intelligence, we can discern when we need outside help, and from where. We may need to ask a real person or read a real book. It may be that the crucial factor is creating it quickly, but what if that isn't the case? What if our Authentic Intelligence is asking us to consider the possibility that speed isn't everything and that the actual practice of being in contact with and a channel for your own Authentic "I" is worth every minute?

Reflection Questions

- What's stopping you from consulting your Authentic "I"?
- Where are you relying on a fake, lying, common AI when you could be relying on a bottomless, honest, unique-to-you AI?
- Where can you get your Authentic "I" lessons?
- What else do you think is possible here?

CHAPTER 2

How We Know Now

Joan of Arc is frequently credited with this brilliant reply when the judge accused her of being the victim of her own imagination: 'How else would God speak to me?'

— RICHARD ROHR[3]

The time when we routinely cede our power and authority to others is coming to an end. In the past few years, accelerated by the pandemic, many Americans have joined the rest of the world in leaving behind organized religion and teachings. This is not a prediction. This is not a hope. In the U.S. alone, led by the Baby Boomers before them, the Millennial and Gen Z generations are not only fleeing organized religion but also using the internet's technology to disrupt conventional structures and platforms.

In today's world, we can't always agree on who to trust or listen to. If we have a conscious relationship with a higher power, we may no longer rely on ministers, priests, rabbis, or imams to help us know what God thinks. In "spiritual but not religious" contexts, where we place a premium on the right to choose and the ability to directly

3 *The Universal Christ* by Richard Rohr

access Spirit, we often fail to teach or learn *how* to discern. For example, in 12-step recovery groups, the literature says, "We pray only for God's will for us and the power to carry that out." However, it doesn't specify how to discern God's will for us.

However much we love our parents, partners, or friends, we may not feel we can turn to them with the hardest questions we have. When we present our choices to members of our (chosen) family, they may be unable to separate *their* needs from ours.

Many of us also quickly go down an internet rabbit hole trying to figure out our solution. So many experts on so many platforms claim to know exactly what we need. Whether I'm wrestling with a health, work, sex, relationship, or investment question, surely there is an expert out there to provide the "right" answer.

But how do we choose the right expert? And if their advice is contradictory, how do we know whose advice to follow (and what to pay for and how much)? Choosing a restaurant is one thing; choosing a life partner, deciding on a home to buy, or following a specific health protocol is another.

Reflection Questions

- Who do you turn to now for answers to your most important questions?
- Is it your friends, family members, or AI/the Internet?
- Is it a trusted advisor outside of that?
- What questions do you have about your ability to go within for your answers?

CHAPTER 3

The Importance of Knowing

True education is not pumped and crammed in from outward sources, but aids in bringing to the surface the infinite hoard of wisdom within.

— RABINDRANATH TAGORE

You probably noticed that the title of this book contains the word *know* twice. That's because both are necessary. It is not enough to *know* (what's true for me, what's light, what's expansive, what matches my vision of my life, my destiny). All of us have the capacity and the ability to *know*. Or, put more simply, we all do *know*. But do we *know* that we know? Answer: another "no."

Some have substituted *faith* for *knowing*. When we have *faith,* it implies that we trust a deity "knows" and is watching over us, keeping us safe, but that we ourselves do not have access to that perspective or consciousness. We ourselves must simply have *faith* that someone or something else outside of us is tuned in and taking care of business.

This handbook is for people who *know* what they know but want to know even more, for people who don't *know* what they know and are eager to discover what's possible, and it's for everyone in between.

In it, we'll evaluate how *knowing* we are in a variety of areas, from food to sex to politics; we'll look at what has kept us from *knowing* so far, and we'll explore some tools for *knowing*.

Some of the things that have kept us from *knowing* are "toxic mimics" of *knowing*, so we'll get into that soon.

You'll also have the opportunity to explore your own streams of knowing, discovering which ones flow strongly and which may be dammed up. Are you clear what's yours to create (draw, write, sing, build), but not what's yours to eat? Are you flowing in work, but not in relationships? You'll have an opportunity to get to *know* yourself at a deeper level and find out where there's room for your streams of *knowing* to flow more strongly.

What Can Inner Knowing Bring to Your Life?

In a time before the internet...Chuck and Debbie were driving across New York state to meet a group of us camping in the Adirondacks. The country roads on that route hit small town after small town. When they drove through the village of Minerva, Chuck got excited.

> "Debbie, wake up, we're driving through Minerva."
>
> "Um, okay, I'm awake. Minerva? So what, Chuck?"
>
> "You don't get it, Debbie. We're in Minerva. We've *finally reached Minerva.*"
>
> "Chuck, I think I know what you mean, but I don't think you got that right. I can't remember what people want to *reach*, but I don't think it's Minerva!"

When Chuck and Debbie got to the campground, Chuck hopped out and told the story. A bunch of us ribbed him,

> "It's Nirvana, Chuck, Nirvana!" And, "Chuck, we know you. You may have reached the state of *Minerva*, but you definitely have yet to reach *Nirvana*."

It got me thinking that, as human beings, particularly living in Western developed nations, we may spend most of our time living in a state of *Minerva*, even when we aspire to a state of *Nirvana*.

What and where is the state of Minerva?

While the concept of "Minerva to Nirvana" was suggested to me by my friend Chuck's amusing mistake, it's worth noting that Minerva is also a Goddess of wisdom, war, strategy, and commerce. The "state of Minerva" and the main qualities associated with the Goddess Minerva can be compared to the part of the mind accessed through the left hemisphere of the brain. In addition to the troubling parts attributed to the goddess, the left brain is also where many of the most useful and rewarded parts of the human experience live: the to-do list, goal setting, the ability to take and complete actions, not to mention analytical thinking. Minerva was said to have sprung from her father Jupiter's head full-sized and fully clothed in armor–presumably also defensive and afraid (why would she have needed armor if she didn't perceive herself to be under attack?)

What and where is the state of Nirvana?

Nirvana is the place we are standing when we *know* what we *know*. In Nirvana, we exist beyond the constraints of time and space.

We are connected to all of consciousness. We are plugged into the all-knowing, all-powerful, ever-present. All lack, limitation, worry, doubt, and fear are gone. All separation from others is gone. All judgment is gone.

It's also where creativity lives: new ideas, painting, music, humor, writing, and design.

The state of Nirvana can be accessed through the right side of the brain, or, as some would also add, the pineal gland of the brain. While some may seek to attain a permanent state of Nirvana, most of us visit it only for short periods of time in a day or week, or maybe even once in a lifetime, maybe only as we transition out of the human experience at death.

How do we move from Minerva To Nirvana?

I've studied, practiced, and taught multiple vehicles that can reliably get us across the bridge from Minerva to Nirvana. My special focus has been on understanding and applying the quantum physics of consciousness through learning and integrating various tools.

Two of my favorite passwords to enter the gates of Nirvana (to say when in a state of Minerva) are "What else is possible?" and "How does it get any better than this?"[2] These are questions best uttered aloud. Those questions can move us from Minerva to Nirvana by inviting the universe to show us something we hadn't yet considered. Nothing needs to go on our to-do list other than curiosity – what else *is* possible? What am I not seeing? What am I not hearing? Where am I so stuck in lack and limitation and the apparent reality that I cannot perceive, know, be, or receive any other possibility?

2 Access Consciousness tools

Can Everyone Know?

The short answer is yes. Knowing (as distinguished from "knowledge," which would be the normal noun to use for the verb *to know*) is not about book learning or study or research or figuring it out. Knowing is about connecting to a part of ourselves that knows and knows that it knows.

Does everyone know?

We all have that potential. Every being, from a blade of grass to a rock on the planet, is part of the cosmic democracy and has some form of awareness. It may not be quite the same as what human beings mean when we say the word "know" (but then again, it may be). Every human being is a conscious being having a conscious experience on a human plane. As such, we are connected with universal consciousness and have the potential to know much of what it knows. Since universal consciousness is beyond time, space, and constraints, there is a part of us that exists beyond the apparent limits of time and space. It is more a state of being than something we can acquire. We already know, but do we know that we know?

Can everyone choose from what they know?

Does everyone choose from their inner knowing? The answer is no. Most of us choose based on many other factors.

Can everyone choose based on that *knowing*? Yes. We are all built with the hardware and software to access it. This may be one of those things that we, as babies and small children, come ready-equipped to do but get trained out of. This book provides the ability to get trained back in.

Can your knowing be trained out of you?

I don't think your inner knowing ever leaves. The ability to know is there. However, it is possible to be trained into thinking that it's dangerous for us to know or that we should avoid knowing. For centuries, women, people of color, anyone who was not being drawn to the dominant religion or political or cultural or structural order was trained first by their families (to keep them safe from arrest or violent consequences) and then by society if their families didn't do that job.

In some cultures, social strata, or economic levels, it can feel safe to *know*. Others might be taught to secretly *know* but not to show it.

Many today, even in societies that claim to be free, are subject to emotional, physical/sexual abuse as children that may have the effect of convincing the survivors that it isn't safe for them to *know* what they know. In my experience, recovering with survivors of such trauma, the ability to *know* is never diminished. All the hardware and software are still there, knowing and hoping that we can, at some point, *know that we* know.

There is a lot of belief in today's circles that it takes years of therapy to release the trauma patterns that can disrupt so many areas of life. That wasn't my experience. Years of therapy actually did little to help me change or grow or access knowing.

The long road to recovery is a 20th-century belief. Multiple modalities are circulating in the 21st century, which, like everything else about the era, work quickly and easily. Science of Mind, of which I am a student, longtime practitioner, and minister, is a quick-change tool that early 20th-century people decided needed years to learn (does it, though?). Access Consciousness, which I have also studied, is a quick-change tool that can be learned in almost no time. The

Access people know this, but they also know there's a lot more money to be made from taking a lot of classes to get "certified."

We're going to explore some tools in this book that are easy ways to *know* that we know. And at the end of the book, you can also find some of my other favorite tools for changing our perception of reality.

What can we know?

Oh, so much. We can know what food or treatments are most beneficial for our bodies. We can tune into our true heart's desire in love relationships. We can know whether to buy or sell homes and other assets. We can know whether to cooperate with or resist an autocratic regime. We can know what our life's work is and how to make a difference.

What if we have wisdom and support right inside us?

Almost everything we read about this concept of "God" suggests that He/She/It/They are outside of us. The very inquiry into *discernment* or divine guidance reinforces that idea. It's almost like there's me over here living my life, and then there's God over there. Hmm, maybe I would be better off if I "went over there and talked and listened to God."

I believe that God (whether it is called He, She, It, They, Allah, Elohim, the sacred grandmother tree, the Atman-Brahman presence, the unified field, the Father, Son, the Holy Ghost, or just plain Love) is omniscient, omnipotent, and omnipresent. That means It is everywhere; therefore, it does stand to reason that It is "over there." But that also means that *It* is "over here." It is right where I am. It is a part of me.

What occurs to me, and I'm sure that I'm not the first to observe this, is that when I don't choose to turn to the part of myself connected with universal intelligence, I truly reject the full power of myself and my gifts. It is as if I have functional upper and lower intestines, and I decide I only need my lower intestine. I'll just have my upper intestine removed since I don't understand what it does and have never seen it.

Science tells us there is a unified field that makes up all things. I am connected to that field. Because I am connected to it, I have access to knowledge, support, and assistance that is beyond my senses if I choose to avail myself of it. It is right here where I am, available and living it's perfect life in and as and through me. Plus, it is also right over there.

Reflection Questions

- Have you been living from what you should do today or from what else is possible?
- What might it be like to spend more time in a sensation of connection with all things?
- What if you are always guided and loved?
- At this point, do you feel more like Minerva (left brain/thinking) or more like Nirvana (right brain/feeling)?

CHAPTER 4

Why Don't We Know?

You don't need faith when you know.
You need faith when you don't know.

— REV. RICK HARRELL

Although my parents (born in the United States in the 1930s) were free thinkers in their time, they didn't teach me how to dial into my inner wisdom. I was encouraged to *think* for myself but not to *know* for myself. The distinction between *thinking* and *knowing* is important. Up until 2016, in this relatively free period in world and American history, thinking for oneself was theoretically valued. Creative content such as writing literature, creating art or fun, exciting, amusing social media was rewarded and celebrated.

Anytime someone dials into their creative force, they know what they know. Anytime someone writes and brings forth something new, they know what they know. Predominantly, we are taught how to think and what to think. "Creatives" are often unusual people among us. We like what they do, and we buy it, but we insist that we are not that. How often has someone said, "I'm" not creative"?

How I Learned That I Know

When our kids were about 5 and 6, I had the chance to take my first "just mommy" trip without them or my husband. Around that time, my neighbor offered a "No Accidents, No Mistakes" painting and yoga weekend workshop.

I was no artist, but I liked Mego, the instructor. I was starting to get into yoga, and this was inexpensive, the right weekend, price, and location.

Mego gives us each a large white sheet of butcher paper and a bunch of brushes. She tells us that we will be working in the medium of tempera, which, it turns out, is not Japanese batter-fried vegetables, but a type of paint that dries quickly and covers up other paint easily. This will allow us to paint freely without constraint or judging our work or overthinking. She promises that whatever happens happens, and we can easily just paint over it.

Ever since my second-grade teacher put my art (and seemingly no one else's) in the trash can, when anyone brings out art supplies, I leave the building or I leave my body. This trip is no exception. It gets worse. It turns out the other four painters are professionals, so they dive in. I sit there, not a speck of paint yet applied to the canvas, my mind searching for something, anything I can credibly paint. Everyone else has painted so much that they've added new white sheets to their canvas to create more room.

By 10 pm, the rest of the gang is grooving on their huge, glorious projects, and I have yet to lift a brush. I go to bed. I paint nothing the next morning either. They paint a lot. I am bored and angry at myself for blowing my precious free time this way.

About an hour into what promises to be a Saturday evening from hell, maybe around 8 pm, it occurs to me that I have no trouble creating in any other medium. Put me in a room and tell me to write or do improv, and I'll write or improvise for hours. Ask me to compose a song, maybe even design a building, none of which I've done before, and I'll do them and have fun with it. But painting, I just can't do.

Then a new thought parachutes into my mind: perhaps I couldn't really "do" those creative exercises either. If there is some part of me that knows how to write and do, even though *I* do not, maybe there is a part of me that knows how to paint too!

So I ask the part of me that knows how to write and create other things to paint for me and through me. A thought directs me to pick this brush and this color and apply it to this part of the canvas. Then another direction comes. Then another. From this point on, I'm on fire with the creative experience of painting. I create a huge tree, then add on a panel above to reveal a fish, and then another fish (turns out the fish are making out). I love all of it; I have complete energy, and I stay up until like 4 am, covering the canvas bit by bit. The next morning, while everyone else is packing up to go and hugging, I'm still painting. I take the painting home and pay a small fortune to have it framed. It hangs today in our stairwell (because this is the only wall of the house tall enough to accommodate the work). After the painting had been up for a few weeks, our four-year-old daughter said this,

> "Mommy, your painting is changing the whole house."
>
> "How is that, Emily?" I ask.
>
> "Because you couldn't paint, and you made a beautiful painting. Your painting is telling us all that we can do things we think we can't do."

How "Shoulding" On Myself Got In the Way of Knowing

Another reason that people often don't know what we know is that we get taught that what's important is what we *should* do, not what we are shown to do.

As the oldest of three, hyper-responsibility came with the territory. When I was two, my baby brother died in his sleep. Unconsciously, to avoid the next tragedy, I appointed myself in charge of saving my next two brothers. Our mother, while also loving and caring, was erratic in aspects of caregiving like getting dinner on the table or providing timely transportation or, well, anything. So, I decided that, for the good of the family, I had to be clear about what needed to be done and when.

With this very early experience, even the smallest decisions took on a life-or-death quality. If I chose the wrong thing or failed to act, in my young mind, someone might die. Some part of little Sara (me) decided that she needed to figure out what should be done and do it. She and she alone shouldered responsibility for the safety of her family (if not the world).

Mistaken belief:

Heavy = Should

Should = Yes

The Truth:

Light = Yes

Heavy = No

So, when I was introduced to the tool called "What is Light for You?" (which you'll soon learn), I discovered I had a problem. At first, it was much easier to discern heavy than light, and heavy felt like a yes to me because heavy equaled should and should equaled yes.

Whenever someone would ask, "Is this light or heavy? Is this true?" I would stare at them like a raccoon caught in headlights. (Raccoons, unlike deer, have an agenda; mine was doing what I *should* do as a way to survive.)

I finally figured out why. Obligations (like old ideas) may constrict our chest and throat because they bind us to them. So the idea of feeling what is light, free, expansive, and non-constrictive is radical and dangerous for some people, and was for me. How dare I even be interested in, let alone do, what feels light? We are supposed to do what we *should* do, duh! In my case, my lifelong unconscious belief that heavy equaled must and light equaled impossible was perpetuating a life of resentment and stuckness.

Reflection Questions

- What's one way you sense your body's innate wisdom?
- How do you access it?
- What's the best thing you believe about your body?
- Who is light to support you in that?

CHAPTER 5

The Toxic Mimics of Knowing

Being still inexperienced and having just made conscious contact...it is not probable that we are going to be inspired at all times. We might pay for this presumption in all sorts of absurd actions and ideas.

— BILL W.[3]

In Western culture, many other mental applications masquerade as knowing. In this chapter, we will examine those and compare them to true knowing. At times, one or more of these applications may be life-saving, but when they show up at the mental costume party dressed as *knowing*, they can be toxic to our ability to discern our truth. So let's explore them one by one.

The 1st Toxic Mimic of Knowing: Thinking

Dr. Dain Heer said, "Thinking is a lower harmonic of knowing." That means that thinking is not the same as knowing. Thinking is, as we talked about in Minerva to Nirvana, a left-brained activity.

3 (The "Big Book" of) *Alcoholics Anonymous*

Thinking is working mostly with the information already on our brain's hard-drive, or what we perceive with our senses. It does not access the universal cloud storage of knowing.

False belief: I think therefore I know

An example of *thinking* would be when we are looking for a job. Most of us, when we want to find a job, look at what we believe to be our skills, and then decide what type of job, based on what we've known before (or perhaps a quick Google search), and what kind of jobs we're qualified for. And then, based on that thinking, we start to look for known, existing jobs that are advertising. When we apply and aren't hired or worse, we see no jobs advertised of the kind we *think* we're qualified for, we decide that there are no jobs for us. Therefore, using rational deduction (which is just thinking with a fancy name), we conclude that we will not get a job that we're qualified for or want.

An example of *knowing* as opposed to *thinking* in this scenario would be when my husband and I bought a home on the other side of the country without having jobs in the city of our new home (in a time before widespread remote working). At that time, there was a nationwide economic downturn. I expressed a worry to my husband about moving to another city without a job offer in hand. I cited a statistic in the newspaper stating that a high percentage of people spent up to six months looking for jobs in our sector. He asked, "Honey, is there a percentage of people who DO get jobs in our sector quickly?" I said, "Yeah, there's a percentage, it's like 3 percent." He said, "Then that's our percentage. We're the 3 percent."

This wasn't arrogance on my husband's part. It wasn't an affirmation. This was my husband expressing his own *knowing*. He's a smart guy. He knows how statistics work. He simply knew that we were on the best end of those statistics. Instead of *thinking* about whether we'd get a job and how we'd get one, he just *knew* we would. (See *Know Your Beliefs* for more about this.)

And, indeed, we moved and in a matter of weeks, I secured a high-paying job with great benefits.

The 2nd Toxic Mimic of Knowing: Remembering

Remembering may be evolutionarily advantageous, but it is not the same as knowing. With good reason, a lot of us mistake remembering for knowing. We're a highly successful species on the planet because we remember. For thousands of years, the human brain has kept us safe by remembering where the venomous snakes or sabertooth tigers hang out, and how to avoid, disable, or kill them so that we can stay alive.

False belief: I remember so I don't have to know

When we lived in more challenging times, constantly facing multiple physical threats, this ability to remember and avoid past mistakes set us apart from other species, allowing us to survive and thrive. In modern life in a developed nation, this translates into repeating the past instead of living our best now.

Maybe the last time we went dancing, the club was overcrowded, over-expensive, or it was during a pandemic. We used to love dancing, but the evolutionarily protective part of our brain tells us, "We don't go out dancing anymore, it isn't safe." So we just take that off the table of our lives.

Perhaps if we connect with the part of us that *knows,* we may discover whether this particular time, place, and manner of dancing would be a light and expansive option for us, rather than simply *remembering* a time that it wasn't.

Or, to use a more globally impactful example of *knowing*, for the first couple of hundred thousand years of homo sapiens they lived in harmony with nature, and their fuel sources remained plentiful and replenished. At some point after we developed "civilization," we started to cultivate and burn fuel sources such as wood and coal, and eventually oil and gas, as though they were infinite in supply. While it has always been evident that the burning of fuel pollutes the air and depletes resources, those who controlled these resources were enriched by their use and continued to do so.

At some point, it became impossible for anyone to question or stop this trajectory of development and expansion. Yet, at the time I write, it has become apparent to most of the world that the path we're on is leading to the destruction of human and other habitats and therefore unsustainable (and close to irreversible).

In other words, *remembering* that the way to prosperity and energy is burning fossil fuels instead of *knowing* that there are different ways to produce energy and prosperity is threatening our very existence.

Knowing instead of *remembering* may save our lives.

The 3rd Toxic Mimic of Knowing: Worry

Worry is negative future planning. A close cousin of remembering, which focuses on the past, worry focuses on the future. As Ernest Holmes put it, "all thought is creative and influential." Including when we worry. Worry is a form of negative fantasy. When we worry, we are using our powerful creative minds to focus intensely on a worst-case scenario. We are asking ourselves questions about the future and then imagining the answers to them. What if someone dies or gets injured? What if the stock market crashes? What if the candidate I fear and despise gets elected president? What if I am humiliated by choosing this path instead of another?

False belief: I worry so that I'll prepare for the worst

Many successful people know that whatever we put our attention on is more likely to manifest than what we don't. Therefore, it makes sense to focus consciously on what we want, rather than what we don't like. Yet, many of us also worry, which is exactly the opposite.

Some take it a step further and choose pessimism as a life strategy. My mother was one of these. She felt that it was best to prepare for the worst by imagining the worst. Mom's negative focus on the future may have taught me more about the importance of mind control than anything else she could have modeled. As a young child, I grasped that a life of expecting the best would lead to greater happiness for me than one of expecting the worst. I even came up with a crude math to prove that optimism is a better life choice than pessimism.

As an adult who is more in touch with my inner knowing than I once was, I am actually able to relax more. It turns out that my optimistic approach was a form of control. Unable to accept my mom's worry, I fiercely focused on its opposite. In more recent years, I have learned that, whether I am pushing against the negative and towards the positive or leaning from the positive to the negative, all polarities trap me in the present reality rather than open me to *what else is possible*.

Knowing is what pops me from worry into peace, surrender, and joy. It offers a simple way to allow and choose that which matches the feeling I want.

The 4th Toxic Mimic of Knowing: Fear

Fear is essential and necessary, but it can also make it impossible for us to know. All feelings are arrows pointing in the direction of healing. So fear, as a feeling, can play a key role in guiding us to knowing. However, it often doesn't succeed because fear can act like a computer virus, taking over the system and shutting down the connection.

False belief: Fear points the way to healthy decisions

Fear is frequently the combined result of *thinking*, *remembering*, and *worrying*. *Knowing* often speaks to us in "the still, small voice within" or is felt rather than heard. Fear is generally loud and insistent. It needs to be since its purpose is to save us from harm.

Real fear triggers the body's fight-or-flight response, activating and releasing stress hormones throughout our system. When we are in fear, we lose the ability to even think, let alone *know*. Our brains actually shut down the thinking part so that we recruit everything we have to defend ourselves (fight), run (flight), play dead (freeze), or pacify our attacker (faun).

It's generally impossible to have a helpful conversation with a person who is strongly afraid unless we can do something to alleviate their fear and calm them down.

Sometimes what is now widely known as a "trauma" response can activate this fear system. We talk about "trauma" these days as if the trauma pattern itself is the same as what induced the trauma. Trauma is actually an abiding physical and emotional imprint on the brain and body designed to protect us from going through whatever harm caused the pattern to begin with. In some ways, it is our software for "remembering."

One technique that can work is just a reality check:

Is this fear based on anything real?
Grip the chair you're in.
Look around the room.
Is a wild animal or crazed human in your environment?
Probably not.
Is there a fire, an earthquake, a hurricane? Also, probably not.
Is anyone actually threatening you with a knife, a gun, or other weapon?

If the answer is no, then you are probably safe, and the fear isn't warranted. Now you can use one of the many tools people have for getting out of or completely deactivating fear-causing trauma reactions. I have used eye movement desensitization and reprocessing (EMDR) therapy, Emotional Freedom Technique (EFT, also known as "tapping"), biofeedback machines, various forms of meditation, and other modalities to arc me from flight or fight (where I can't *know*) back into rest and relaxation (where I can).

The 5th Toxic Mimic of Knowing: Shame & Guilt

Like all other toxic mimics of knowing, shame and guilt seem helpful at first. Isn't it good to review how we've behaved and learn from our mistakes? Absolutely. A daily inventory is a key part of my spiritual practice. However, shame and guilt can mimic and disrupt true knowing precisely because when they occur, they typically feel unavoidable and 100% rationally justified.

False belief: Shame & guilt make me a better person

It's been said that guilt is "I did something bad," while shame is "I am something bad." "I know I did (or am) bad, therefore I feel guilty (ashamed)." I mustn't do or be that again. And I cannot trust myself to connect with inner knowing.

The inquiry into what could have been better isn't the toxic mimic. That's fine. It's the shame and guilt that often accompany that behavioral review that is the problem. Shame and guilt are loud noises that make it hard to tune into the frequency of *knowing*. And while avoiding shame and guilt is an essential human quality that can motivate us to be better neighbors, friends, parents and lovers by acting in alignment with integrity, paradoxically we can spiral into shame where we continue to behave in a way that doesn't serve us which causes us to use whatever we're using to continue to behave that way instead of changing.

Nowhere is this more evident than in living out addictive patterns. Whether we are ashamed of our reliance on painkillers, wine, chocolate, dating apps, shopping, Netflix, or social media, our inability to control or refrain from returning to a given substance or activity may cause shame. When we feel ashamed, we may feel alone and unable to share our struggles with anyone else. "If they knew how I really am, they wouldn't love me" can be a prevalent thought.

I know this because I have lived in the cycle of addiction to certain foods, excitement, and constant activity, and then shame because I once again succumb to those behaviors even though I try hard not to. And then I felt shame again because I had. Rinse and repeat.

This entire cycle, whether it involves just shame or shame combined with substance or activity, can be used to avoid feeling and disrupt our ability to tune into truth.

The 6th Toxic Mimic of Knowing: Doubt

Doubt depends on us believing that, "it's healthy to question everything" to the exclusion of all else. Doubt lives between knowing and not knowing. For our spiritual literacy, doubt is not the opposite of knowing. It is the commonplace experience of knowing but not trusting that we know–vacillating between knowing and not knowing. Because doubt implies, but does not fully embrace, "faith" (which is a cousin to "knowing"), it leaves us in the wind.

False belief: It's arrogant to be sure about anything

To be in doubt is to shimmer in the ambiguity between trusting and not trusting in a universal consciousness. It's possible to trust consciousness without trusting yourself to access it. To know what you know is to both trust consciousness and to trust yourself to be able to reliably access the part of you that is plugged into greater consciousness.

Reflection Questions

- Have you ever used thinking, fear, remembering, worry, or shame as a substitute for knowing?
- What were the circumstances and how has that served you?
- How has that not served you?
- By removing the toxic mimics in those circumstances, how might your inner knowing serve you better?

CHAPTER 6

How Can We Know?

Follow your instincts. That's where true wisdom manifests itself.

— OPRAH WINFREY

What if just by asking any question aloud, we have a reliable body sensation that tells us whether the answer is yes or no?

The question is similar to "What is true for you?"

Primary Tool #1: Light vs. Heavy

If someone asks me, or I ask myself, "Is this true for me?" and I get a "light" feeling, it means the answer is yes. If, on the other hand, I get a constricted, heavy feeling, then the answer is no. This is simple in concept but not easy in reality.

Light (spacious/expansive) = yes

Heavy (stuck/clenched) = no

Can You Try This?

Bring to mind a question. It doesn't have to be a yes or no question, but let's try one:

> *How about I take a weekly tennis lesson on Tuesday evening for the next six weeks?* (Note: Even if you have zero interest in tennis, maybe try using this question. Knowing in advance that the answer is no can help you learn what a "no" feels like.)
>
> *Say aloud, "What will my life feel like in five years if…* (I take a tennis lesson every Tuesday for the next six weeks?)"
>
> I suggest you push it out five years because the conscious mind will not have any idea of the effect that this little choice will have in five years. But the unlimited mind to which we're connected–"your nonlocal intelligence"–is beyond time and space. It knows. By pushing the timeline out absurdly far, we take the thinking out of it and go straight to sensing. (Note the difference between *feel* like and *be* like–we have no way to know what it will *be* like, but maybe we can *feel.*)
>
> *How does that choice feel in your body?*
>
> Put your hand on your chest. Is there a sensation of light, expansiveness, and spaciousness, or does it feel heavy, stuck, and clenched?

Or somewhere in between?

Make a note of or remember that feeling, and now ask the question the other way,

"What will my life feel like (in 5 years) if... (I don't take this tennis lesson every Tuesday for the next 6 weeks?)

Dial into it again: How does this feel? Light, heavy, or somewhere in between?

If the feeling is light about taking the tennis lesson and heavy about not taking it, that's easy. The answer is yes, our spirit, our intuitive self, wants to take the class and will benefit from it. If, however, the feeling is the opposite, heavy on taking it and light on NOT taking it, your intuitive guidance system is showing you not to take it.

If you can't tell the difference, you can keep trying or try another tool. If you can tell the difference, but "heavy" seems more like a yes and "light" seems more like a no to you, you might have an issue I had.

Primary Tool #2: Candle Flame

Another tool that can be used for the exact same daily/hourly/minute-by-minute inquiries as Light vs. Heavy is Candle Flame.

To use it,

picture a candle burning bright in your chest.

Now, if you take choice A, what happens to the candle?

> If you take choice B, what happens to the candle? Generally, if the candle burns brighter and stronger, that's a yes.
>
> If it burns weakly and flickers or goes out, that's a no. Determine whether a choice makes your internal candle flame burn brighter or flicker and go out

This tool can also be used for day-to-day, little and big choices, everything. If Light vs. Heavy doesn't work, this could be your basic *know* tool.

In each section to follow, whether you choose to use or get to know the tool, we suggest you practice your basic tool, either What's Light for Me or Candle Flame.

So before you launch into the next section, maybe make your first "Know what you know" choice by using one of these tools. You're going to have a lot of time to practice this tool, but just right now, please give it a try!

Reflection Questions

- Can you think of a recent event that caused a conflict between your inner feelings and what you saw or experienced?
- Using one of the tools, can you tell the difference between light and heavy yet?
- What can you relate to with should = yes?
- How might it make sense to have light = yes instead?

SECTION

Getting to Know You: Exploring Your Streams of Consciousness

The goal is to move from unconscious incompetence to conscious incompetence to conscious competence to unconscious competence[4]

— NOËL BURCH

We move now into the meat of the book's sandwich, getting to know what you know through various parts of life that everyone has. In each of these sections, you'll have an opportunity to dial into what you know about a specific area of living, thinking, or being. You'll be invited to practice a tool for self-knowing by taking an inventory in that area and sitting with what is true for you. I call this the Stream of Consciousness Inventory. Plus, you'll get to hear some of what I and others have learned about that part of life. Hearing what others think they know can be a phenomenal way to clarify our own understanding.

4 from *The Four Stages of Incompetence*

Each of these inventories offers a chance to *know* (or face) something more about ourselves than we did before. It's not so much about uncovering talents, strengths, and weaknesses; it's about making the unconscious conscious as a gateway to healing. Until we know what we know, we're operating in the dark.

In a minute, you'll have an opportunity to take your first inventory. Although this is a bit of a quiz, it's not like any quiz you've ever taken. Throughout these chapters, you're going to be using Light vs. Heavy or the Candle Flame tools that you just learned as your way to test the truth of the inventory statements and practice using these tools.

CHAPTER 7

Know Your Body & Healing

The body has a super wisdom within it that is biased toward health rather than toward the disease.

— CATHERINE PONDER

Why You Need to Know Your Body

We live, move, and have our being inside our bodies, yet many of us know more about our bank accounts than we do about this physical form which we were assigned at birth. This section will look at what best serves our bodies, what healers to consult, and when to implement their suggestions.

Stream of Consciousness Inventory: Find Your FLOW# and Your GROW# to Understand Your Body and Healing Stream Power

To find out how aware you are of your Body & Healing stream flows, use your primary tool (Light vs. Heavy or Candle Flame) to rate each statement below on a scale of 1 to 5 according to how true that statement is for you. 5 indicates the statement is totally true/

light (so it could feel very light and expansive, that's our yes/truth), and 1 indicates that it is false/heavy (so it could feel very heavy and stuck, that's our no/false). Add up your first five ratings to get your FLOW # and the second set of five ratings to get your GROW #. Subtract your GROW# from your FLOW # to get your current Body and Healing Stream Power.

Assign a number to each statement below on how true/light the statement feels for you, 5 being the most true/light, 1 being the most false/heavy.

___ I am in tune with my body's wellness.

___ When I have long-term pain or chronic conditions, I know how best to support myself in healing/living my best possible life.

___ I am clear about which physicians to consult (whether mainstream or alternative), so I follow their instructions.

___ I know whether what physicians/practitioners suggest is valid and valuable advice for me.

___ I can actually listen and communicate with the physically ailing parts of me.

For the five statements above, calculate your **FLOW #** _____

Keep listening to your body. It will tell you when something is not okay.

— EMILY INFELD

Now you're doing the same thing again with a set of statements that come from the other direction. Again, assign a number to each statement below on how true/light the statement feels for you, 5 being the most true/light, 1 being the most false/heavy.

___ I am moving too fast to really know what's going on with my body.

___ I just go to the doctor and do what they say. I never really think about what I know about my body and health.

___ I give up on healing quickly. If one doctor's diagnosis and prescription doesn't cure my issue, I assume I'm stuck with that problem for life. I just need to learn to live with it.

___ I medicate the best I can while I judge, resent, and fear the trajectory of my long-term pain and chronic conditions.

___ I see disease as a path for me to follow to healing.

For the five statements above, calculate your **GROW #** _____

Subtract your GROW # from your FLOW # to find out your KNOW # for your Body and Healing.

FLOW - GROW = _______ KNOW

If your KNOW # is 17-25, congratulations, you know your body; you know how to determine what healing you need and who to consult. You just might be a Super Streamer of Body & Healing.

If your KNOW # is 8-16, you have some confidence in your ability to know your body and your healing choices, but maybe you could use some help trusting yourself more.

If your KNOW # is from less than 0 to 7, it could be an indication that you are somewhat alienated from your body and soul's wisdom about Body & Healing.

Now that you've experimented with Light vs. Heavy and have a sense of where you are with your Body & Healing, maybe you want to try another tool, which I have found to be the most helpful with bodies.

What I've learned about Body & Healing

Thoughts, the mind's energy, directly influence how the physical brain controls the body's physiology...Beliefs control biology!

— BRUCE H. LIPTON[5]

Doctors know a lot, but we do too. In North America, when we experience a persistent health problem, we go to see our doctor, most likely with the credential "M.D." after their name. We bring them our complaints, and they match those symptoms up with possible diseases. Maybe they test various bodily fluids or take our temperature, blood pressure, or other indications that point to a certain disease. Once diagnosed, we're told how to treat that disease, more often than not how to alleviate the symptoms of that disease and live with it because they don't know how to cure it.

5 *The Biology of Belief: Unleashing the Power of Consciousness, Matter & Miracles* by Bruce H. Lipton.

That process can work well. When we are diagnosed on the road to diabetes, medical providers can provide us with insulin, a suggested food plan, or maybe a better way to monitor our blood sugar. Surgery can be the right way to correct a condition. All of those prescriptions might work.

But what about the times the medical profession fail and they can't diagnose a disease, or they can diagnose one but can't cure it? Take Irritable Bowel Syndrome, for example. What about the myriad of autoimmune or related diseases? Lupus, Rheumatoid Arthritis, Multiple Sclerosis, Graves', Crohn's, and fibromyalgia – this ever-growing list causes painful, debilitating symptoms for which there is sometimes alleviating treatment but often no known cure. These diseases disproportionately strike women who frequently are expected to just "live with it," even though they can be disabled by them.

And then there's unexplained pain and limb malfunctions. Long after an injury should have healed, or perhaps without a known injury or cause, myriad people suffer terribly from chronic pain. For a while, the medical "solution" was over-prescription of opioids, which resulted in widespread addiction and tragedy.

So this is why we need to know what is true for our bodies. The stakes are high. And we do know much more than we've been led to believe. We are spiritual beings entrusted with residency in a specific human body. Yet, we've been taught that when it comes to health, we're just "animals" and that our physicians know more about our specific bodies than we do.

Disbelieve in the reality of sickness even when you are ill; an unrecognized visitor will flee!

— PARAMAHANSA YOGANANDA

In Western culture, when we are sick or in pain or have anything wrong with our body, we usually turn to MDs to tell us what is wrong and how to fix it. And often as not, those same MDs, while they might technically make a diagnosis, do not prescribe a cure but prescribe treatment for symptoms.

To be clear: I see allopathic (MDs), osteopathic (DOs), and chiropractic (DCs) physicians on a regular basis. I submit to conventional diagnostic tests. I get surgery when I need to. I take medications as prescribed, sometimes only to treat symptoms. And I also see less traditional healers, like craniosacral, homeopathic, Reiki, psychic healers, and the like. But in my many years of consulting healers of all types and supporting others who are doing the same, I have seen that there are many conditions mainstream medicine and even nontraditional medicine have trouble diagnosing or treating, such as many autoimmune disorders, chronic pain conditions, gastrointestinal and mental health issues, all of which may coincide.

When they can't get to the bottom of what's going on with me (or, worse, seem to have quit trying), why might I assume that the physician has access to more information about my body than I do? It's curious how difficult it can be for some people to even consider listening to their own body. I've met people who happily use spiritual tools to heal their bank accounts but think the same tools and powers won't work on their bodies.

I respect that medical diagnosis of the body requires years of education and experience. And I am not an expert in any aspect of health or medical care. *However,* I AM an expert in me. The way I see it, my Spirit is entrusted with the care and guidance of this human mammal we call the body. I have lived in and with this body for however many years, and I know what has served it and what has not.

Therefore, I have direct access to hearing what my body needs that no one else can.

What can you do to know your Body & Healing?

A tool to try: BODY DIALOGUE — Speaking and listening to your body or a body part to discern what it really needs, and benefit from its wisdom.

How to Use it: Listening to your body can be as simple as this: Sit with a journal or voice recorder handy and your hand (if possible) on the part of the body in discomfort, or that you associate with the discomfort. Say aloud, "What are you trying to tell me? What wisdom do you have for me"? And then making note of it.

Why, Where & When to Use it: Any time you have a persistent physical ailment that your usual remedies don't shift. Obviously, don't wait to talk to a health professional, but if that doesn't work or while you're waiting to get in to see them, why not check out what wisdom is available for you right at hand (maybe literally)?

A story about applying this tool: Another question is, "What do you need from me?" The answers can completely defy logic or reason, but may be worth exploring. I have had lots of conversations with my right knee over the years as it has gone in and out of full function. One time, many years ago, my knee told me quite clearly it needed me to stop wearing shoes with heels. That made sense, so I did that. However, the pain didn't subside. So I asked again. This time it said, "Get all your high heels out of the house." I wasn't wild about that because I thought I might wear heels for special occasions, but I obeyed, gave away a dozen pairs, and then put just a few, maybe six pairs, in our offsite storage closet just in case. Still, the pain didn't go away. I asked again, and my knee said, "When I said offsite, I meant you don't own them anymore. Why would you keep something that harms you?" So I gave them *all* away. Immediately, my pain was gone, and I was able to walk with ease again. Yes, it makes no sense. Who cares?

If you have a troubled body part and an untroubled one, perhaps start a dialogue between those two body parts to see what you get!

Affirmation

I AM INTELLIGENCE.
EVERY PART OF MY BODY IS FILLED WITH DIVINE INTELLIGENCE.
I AM WHOLE, WELL, HARMONIOUS THROUGH AND THROUGH.

Remember, you always have a choice. If you're shown that you should always listen to doctors and do what they say, no matter what, then that is what is for your highest good. Doctors are part of the loving consciousness that is there to support you.

Reflection Questions

- How do you recognize your innate wisdom?
- How do you can access it?
- What's the best thing you believe about your body?
- Who is light to support you in that?

CHAPTER 8

Know Your Creativity

Creativity lives in paradox: serious art is born from serious play.

— JULIA CAMERON[6]

Why You Need to Know Your Creativity

Creativity is a key energy of life as well as a tool for accessing our inner knowing. Yet, unless we're consciously artists or children, many of us give little thought to our creative flow or whether or why we're accessing it. In *The Artist's Way*, Julia Cameron shows us why and how to access our creative flow.

Every one of us is a creative being, whether we're conscious of it or not. Our creativity may be expressed in a conventional way, such as painting, drawing, writing, or composing music; or it may express itself as silly games with children, carpentry, gardening, home decorating, or in our work life.

Although we are creative beings, we may not be allowing space or time for our creativity to flow. That's dangerous, says Julia Cameron.

---

6 From *The Artist's Way*

"Creativity is oxygen for our souls," she also notes. "Cutting off our creativity makes us savage. We react like we are being choked."

Yet, many people think of creativity as something optional or perhaps frivolous that they did as a child, or will do while on vacation, or in retirement, but don't have time for now. So the nudge here is to remember what your creative jam is and where you are dancing with it.

Stream of Consciousness Inventory: Creativity

Learn to accept the possibility that the universe is helping you with what you are doing.

— JULIA CAMERON

To find out how powerfully your Creativity stream flows, rate each statement below on a scale of 1 to 5 according to how true/light that statement is for you. 5 indicates the statement is totally true/light, and 1 indicates that it is false/heavy. Add up your first five ratings to get your FLOW # and the second set of five ratings to get your GROW #. Subtract your GROW # from your FLOW # to get your current Creativity Stream Power.

Assign a number to each statement below on how true/light the statement feels for you, 5 being the most true.

___ I set aside time every day for creative activity.

___ I know where my creative talents lie.

___ Whether it's writing, drawing, playing or singing music, whittling or something else entirely, I set aside regular time to let myself create.

___ I trust that whatever comes through me is worth coming through.

___ I take myself on playdates to music, art, or whatever floats my boat.

For the five statements above, calculate your **FLOW #** _____

Creativity is a spiritual practice.
It is not something that can be perfected,
finished and set aside.

— JULIA CAMERON

___ I am not the creative type.

___ I am creative but there's no way I have time for that.

___ The things that come through me are not worth expressing.

___ I don't have money, time or people to go with on "playdates."

___ Not everyone is creative.

For the five statements above, calculate your **GROW #** _____

Subtract your GROW # from your FLOW # to find out your KNOW # for your Creativity.

FLOW - GROW = _______ KNOW

Congratulations to you for taking the time to know this aspect of yourself. You now know so much more about what you know and what you don't know about Creativity.

If your KNOW # is 17-25, your stream of consciousness on Creativity has a powerful flow.

If your KNOW # is 8-16, your stream of consciousness on this topic is steady but could be stronger if that's something you'd like.

If your KNOW # is from less than 0 to 7, your stream of consciousness on this topic is at a trickle.

What I've learned about Creativity

Enthusiasm is not an emotional state. It is spiritual commitment, a loving surrender to our creative process, a loving recognition of all creativity around us.

—JULIA CAMERON

As detailed earlier, past experiences convinced me that I wasn't an artist and couldn't do anything like "art." Yet, as my story attests, even I was able to access a guiding voice inside me that could do art through me even as I couldn't do it myself. I couldn't have been more alienated from the part of me (that right-brained, Nirvana part) that could paint.

My other creative propensities—such as making up songs, theatre improv and just plain silliness—showed me I could access those sparks, even in a medium that repulsed me.

Some of us strongly believe we have no creative side. Often, we have gathered a lot of evidence for that proposition. We've noticed, perhaps, that we don't have a place of "imagination" or "visualization" in our minds. We may even have received diagnoses that validate this belief. Even now, some readers are arguing with me in their heads. "She's a writer. She has no idea what it means not to be creative."

Well, um, even that argument in our head is quite creative and imaginative. Indeed, it strikes me that one of our most obvious toxic mimics of creativity (see chapter 5, "Toxic Mimics of Knowing") is our ability to MSU.[7] If you've ever found yourself saying or thinking "they threw me under the bus," "they abandoned me," or "they gaslighted me," chances are you're making it up. Not only is there no bus or gaslight involved, but there is also likely no evidence of deliberate betrayal, abandonment, or systematic manipulation in order to make you feel crazy. That doesn't mean it's not happening; it just may not be as deliberate as we believe because our ability to come up with a story about what's happening based on flimsy evidence is staggering. Indeed, employees are so good at making stuff up that corporations are advised to put out frequent notices on upcoming changes to minimize the (highly creative) rumor mill.

My point here is that manufacturing meaning is a creative act. Where does that meaning come from? It is pulled out of the air by my creative spirit. Another way that we humans create (without recognizing that we do so) is through worry or fantasy. Here's the good news and bad news about fantasy: When Olympic or other top athletes are heading into major competitions, they are encouraged to play the game in their mind or see themself "sticking the perfect landing." Why? Because what we picture in our mind fires the exact neural pathways used when we do it in reality. This is why virtual gaming with three-dimensional images is so captivating. The brain doesn't really distinguish between "real" life and fantasy. Fantasy can serve us, like imagining what a world that works for everyone would feel like, a piece of art we'd like to create, or a building or community we'd like to build. We can get that in our head, and then we can bring it into physical reality either through our own actions or by commissioning or inspiring someone else to do so.

7 Make Stuff Up

However, fantasy can also divert us from focusing on what might bring us joy to create. If we're in a committed relationship and fantasizing about liaisons with other people (or consuming pornography), we might call that harmless compared to actual cheating, but a) since the mind knows no difference, it is a form of cheating; b) what we visualize with specificity is more likely to happen in physical reality than what we don't; and c) is this really where we want to put our creative energy?

Since we're all creative beings, how about harnessing the creative force within us to what we would love to create? One way to do that is by *changing the channel* (note, this is not a tool to *know* what you know, but to *use* what you know). When we catch ourselves in unproductive fantasy or worry, or even simply having wandered from the present moment to our to-do list, the day's worst news, or whatever, we can grip something in the room, a piece of furniture or an object, and say to ourselves, "This is real." Then we change the channel and focus on the actual present moment.

Maybe we begin to fantasize about what we would create if we could create anything. If money, time, or talent were no object, what would we create? A painting, a building, a community, a delicious recipe, a birdhouse, a meditation room? What is it? Or, once we know what we know is ours to create, we can begin to change the channel to that, whether in mind or in action or both.

What can you do to know your Creativity?

One of the tools I use the most to know what I know (which is creative in and of itself) is writing. My version of that is what I call 2-Way Writing. This is an absolute staple of *knowing* for me.

A tool to try: 2-WAY WRITING — Writing to your higher intelligence, and having it write back to you, creates an opportunity for dialogue and questions. The Julia Cameron version is just free-flow writing every morning, what she calls "morning pages." I find this version unlocks my innate creativity even better.

How to Use It: This is a go-to tool for me, for sure. Many people will only do this with pen and paper. I prefer a computer when possible, partly because I type really fast and can capture my thoughts better that way. I have a document for the year that I can access at any time, called "Journal." I log in, pull it up, and start writing. This is like a conversation between the ego/small self (Minerva) part of me and the nonlocal intelligence/Higher Self (Nirvana) part of me. Full disclosure: I write to my "Spirit Team," but here I will use "Higher Self" (HS) to make it more widely accessible.

First, I say hello and allow HS to say it back. And then I ask HS one or more questions. Because HS is literally infinitely patient, I've found that it's not like talking to a close friend or family member or even a therapist where they might feel empowered to jump right in with answers, ideas, or advice. Spiritual etiquette requires that we ask for help. This is helpful to me because taking the time to formulate my real questions can be the key to getting answers. Until I know what I'm really asking, I may be unable to receive the answers I need.

Since this is a section about creativity, maybe I'm asking what I should create. Every single step along the way to making this book was a product of knowing what I know and using this or other tools. Depending on where I am in the process of creativity, I might ask HS one or more of these questions.

Sometimes I type out a list of possible things I'm deciding between and just hover my finger over each one and ask in my head, What do you think of this, etc? Sometimes that just gives me a light or heavy feeling, or sometimes words from the HS spring to my fingers. Whatever it is, I write it down.

Other people write longhand in a journal or notebook. Many advise using their dominant hand for their own (self/ego) questions and when responding to the questions as their Higher Self, use their non-dominant hand.

When I try it this way (longhand/switching hands), I usually attempt to copy the words from my Higher Self/Higher Power with my right hand, and perhaps augment/catch the thought that they represent while it's still available to me mentally/emotionally.

There's a decades-old Alcoholics Anonymous adjacent practice of "two-way prayer" with a whole script of phrases to utter to set the stage for the conversation and things to ask one's Higher Self. It's pretty cool, too. A quick internet search will provide a delicious spread of options to learn or practice more about this.

Affirmation

Because spirit is living out its perfect life as me, I am a creative channel in the universe. Spirit speaks, writes, and creates Itself through me and as me.

Reflection Questions

- What's stopping you from admitting that you're a creative being?
- What's your creative jam?
- What did two-way writing help you with?
- What's the next step on the road to creativity for you?

CHAPTER 9

Know Your Life's Work

If you bring forth what is within you, it will save you.
If you do not bring forth what is within you,
it will destroy you.

— THE GNOSTIC GOSPEL OF THOMAS[8]

Psychotherapist and author, Stephen Cope states, "People actually feel happiest and most fulfilled when meeting the challenge of their dharma *in the world*, when bringing highly concentrated effort to some compelling activity for which they have a true calling."

Why you need to "know" your life's work

Dharma is an eastern word with many meanings, including one's true inner calling or life's work. Hindus and Buddhists teach that we all have a dharma, but not all of us are conscious of it or following it. What is our life's work? Are we aware of it? Are we living it? Or are we ignoring an inner calling to our peril?

Many have found their life's work by following a series of coincidences. Some may be rich and famous, but not all people who are

8 Referenced in *The Great Work of Your Life: A Guide for the Journey to Your True Calling* by Stephen Cope

rich and famous are following their dharma, while some people who are toiling in obscurity and relative poverty may be living in blissful alignment with theirs. As Stephen Cope, the author of *The Great Work of Your Life,* puts it, "for me, there is really no longer really any distinction at all between great and ordinary lives."

It's also helpful to know what is really mine to do. Or, put another way, what *could* be mine to do. Every one of us is always at choice in this lifetime. We can be shown what is ours to do and decline to do it. Let's get into it.

Stream of Consciousness Inventory: Your Life's Work

...there is no being in this world without doing.

— STEPHEN COPE

To find out how powerful your Life's Work stream flows, rate each statement below on a scale of 1 to 5 according to how true/light that statement is for you. 5 indicates the statement is totally true/light, and 1 indicates that it is false/heavy. Add up your first five ratings to get your FLOW # and the second set of five ratings to get your GROW#. Subtract your GROW # from your FLOW # to get your current Life's Work Stream Power.

Assign a number to each statement below on how true/light the statement feels for you, 5 being the most true.

___ I am living fully right now.
___ I am bringing forth everything I can bring forth.
___ I am digging down into that ineffable inner treasure-house that I know is in there—that trove of genius.

___ I am living my life's calling.

___ I am willing to go to any lengths to offer my genius to the world.[9]

For the five statements above, calculate your **FLOW #** _____

Those who have a "why" to live can bear with almost any "how."

— VIKTOR E. FRANKL

___ Everyone hates their jobs. I am no exception.

___ I am too busy to know what I enjoy.

___ I don't know what I'm especially good at.

___ "Do what you love and the money will follow" is a myth, no one will pay me to do anything I want to do anyway, so what's the point?

___ So I do whatever job will pay me the most.

For the five statements above, calculate your **GROW #** _____

Subtract your GROW# from your FLOW # to find out your KNOW # for your Life's Work.

FLOW - GROW = _______ KNOW

Congratulations to you for taking the time to know this aspect of yourself. You now know so much more about what you know and what you don't know about Life's Work.

9 Adapted from questions in *The Great Work of Your Life* by Stephen Cope, p. xix

If your KNOW # is 17-25, your stream of consciousness on Life's Work has a powerful flow.

If your KNOW # is 8-16, your stream of consciousness on this topic is steady but could be stronger if that's something you'd like.

If your KNOW # is from less than 0 to 7, your stream of consciousness on this topic is at a trickle.

What I've learned about my life's work

The office was brought for you, and not you for the office.

— PARAMAHANSA YOGANANDA[10]

Almost every profession or job I have had was the product of happenstance or coincidence. Because I learned to type in 4th grade, people paid me to type, which led to a career as a legal secretary after college and a year later, in law school. Because I held a press conference on a slow news day in Washington as part of a law school class, and my little lawsuit got national media attention (and my boyfriend had certain social connections through work), I got hired by Public Citizen as an attorney advocating before Congress. Because one of our children was ill for much of his childhood, I sought much medical and spiritual help for him and for me. Eventually, that path led me to recover from multiple addictive patterns and to become a minister in the Centers for Spiritual Living.

The wrong job can lead to the right work. As I transitioned out of full-time ministry, I got back into public policy, working for the Joint Emergency Management Committee of the legislature and the Assembly Arts and Entertainment Committee. Both were marvelous jobs and experiences until they weren't. One job ended abruptly with

10 *Autobiography of a Yogi* by Paramahansa Yogananda

months of paid leave which propelled/allowed me to write this book. I walk through all this because it shows that many abrupt life changes end up being perceived as positive and necessary after the fact. In his viral TED Talk, author Dan Gilbert suggests we're preprogrammed to be happy with the choices that are forced upon us by life.[11]

The job search starts in our mind (not in the job postings). When people are looking for work, the tendency is to look for advertised openings for positions. Looking for job openings works well for certain types of jobs, such as restaurants and retail. But for so many jobs worth having, even when advertised, by the time we are interviewed, vetted, and considered, the job might already basically be filled. Sometimes the job is filled before it gets posted. But if you think back on your work history (if you don't have a work history, don't worry, the tools work well for this too), how many of the better jobs you've gotten, or perhaps heard about people getting, came from applying to a broadly advertised opening? Most of the time, the better jobs I got were from word of mouth,

Being of service can open the floodgates for receiving. One time, while I was actively looking for a job, I took some time out to help a friend get a piece of public interest legislation passed (the legislation would require that any political advertisement disclose the main funders behind the ad). I didn't perceive that I really had time to do this, but because it was a good cause, I agreed to walk around the state Capitol building with him talking to legislators and staff on behalf of this bill. While I walked around, I ran into several people who remembered me from the last time I had worked in that arena.

11 In his TED Talk on "The Surprising Science of Happiness," Dan Gilbert, challenges the idea that we'll be miserable if we don't get what we want. Our "psychological immune system" lets us feel truly happy even when things don't go as planned. Video available on YouTube.com.

One of them, who represented a powerful organization whose goals I agreed with, spotted me from a hallway, did a double-take, and basically pried the ancient elevator doors open to squeeze on board. He whispers (because you never know who is listening in the Capitol building) that the organization's legislative advocate in my field of experience left and that they needed a replacement, and was I interested? And that, of course, ended up being my job.

What else is possible? Not every sector has places you can walk around, and not everyone knows as many people as I do in their desired sector, so that's not the point of this story. The point of this story is to get curious. One of my favorite tools/prayers is the question "What else is possible?"[12] I mutter "what else is possible," like a maniac, all the time. Basically, I say it every time I think there are no good options, from being stuck in traffic while I'm late to an appointment, to being hit with a huge financial expense, to thinking that I'm unqualified for any job that I would want to do.

The question is not a homework assignment or a to-do list. It's not for me to answer the question, really. It's a question for the universe. My only job is to get curious, pay attention, and keep my eyes open for what is really possible. When I do that, I have ideas, meet people, and discover new possibilities. See the Tool of Coincidence below to see how to and why to pay attention to coincidences during this period.

> *...the seemingly accidental meeting of two unrelated chains in a coincidental event which appears both highly improbable and highly significant.*
>
> — ARTHUR KOESTLER

12 Access Consciousness brought this question to my attention

What can you do to know your Life's Work?

A tool to try: THE TOOL OF COINCIDENCE — Paying attention to and tracking coincidence.

How to Use it: Keep track of coincidences or synchronicities every day somewhere where you can look back at them. The more improbable the coincidence, the more you emphasize it on that list. Periodically look through the list. It's possible that something you didn't fully understand from before will jump out at you later.

Why, Where & When to Use it: Since paying attention to coincidence is communication with your "nonlocal" intelligence, it's a primary Know What You Know tool. When you're at a crossroads, like looking for a job or trying to decide whether to take a relationship to the next level, come back to this list of coincidences and look over it.

How to use it to Know Your Life's Work: As described above, the tool of tracking coincidences is a great one for really falling into your life's work. For the next month, start writing down every coincidence you spot and indicate how improbable it seems. Re-read your entries for the month as a way to read the signposts that your Higher Self has put up for you to see. And in this manner, you will gain a powerful tool for moving forward in your quest for the job that most serves you.

Affirmation

I AM DOING WHAT I AM HERE TO DO, AND I LOVE IT.

Reflection Questions

- If you know your dharma (life's work), what's one step you could take today on that path?
- Even if you don't know, what's one way you could be of service this week?
- What synchronicities or coincidences have you noticed lately?
- In what direction might they be pointing?

CHAPTER 10

Know Your Judgments

If you had no judgments of you, your body, your life, your future, your money, your wealth, or your choices ever again, what would you create?

— GARY DOUGLAS[13]

Why you need to know your judgments

All of us in this culture have judgments against ourselves and others. It often starts with ourselves and radiates forth. We all have judgments, which, when entrenched, can be called biases—the culture we're raised in implants them. The culture I'm raised in has implanted judgments against people with different skin colors than I have (which we call racism); judgments against women (even though I am one, and we call that sexism); judgments against gay, trans, queer, poly and anyone sexually or "gender-ly" different than what I was raised to believe was the right gender or way to be or live that gender (we call that homophobia or transphobia); judgments against non christians (which we might call anti-semitism or islamophobia); judgments against people without education or class (which we call

13 Founder of Access Consciousness

classism) and probably lots more. The culture has also implanted judgments against people who are constantly calling out bias, people who think the way I have habitually spoken or was raised to speak and think isn't okay, and that I need to change. And also judgments against people who have judgments against people who call out bias and judgments. The circle of judgment can seem unending.

There are scores of books out there that will teach you more about all these "isms" and the role that they have played in world or North American history. No doubt it is essential to be alert and on deck to identify when we have a bias or an operating system-level judgment. But since the focus of this book is *How to Know What You Know*, the focus of this section is on the degree to which we are reliable observers of our own minds, and then learning and using a tool for pulling the weeds we call judgments so that we can have a clearer channel to our own knowing.

Stream of Consciousness Inventory: Judgments

When you realize that judgments are not real and they do not contribute to consciousness at all, then you can be, do, and have anything and everything you desire.

— GARY DOUGLAS

To find out how aware you are of your judgments, rate each statement below on a scale of 1 to 5 according to how true/light that statement is for you. 5 indicates the statement is totally true/light, and 1 indicates that it is false/heavy. Add up your first five ratings to get your FLOW # and the second set of five ratings to get your GROW #. Subtract your GROW # from your FLOW # to get your current Judgments Awareness Flow.

Assign a number to each statement below on how true/light the statement feels for you, 5 being the most true.

___ I know I have inherent unconscious judgments.
___ I feel so much shame and guilt over my judgments, that I'm reluctant to look at them or admit them.
___ I notice that I constantly judge myself and others (and I am increasingly amused at myself for that).
___ I am willing to extend love and forgiveness to myself and others despite our judgments.
___ Whether I'm aware of my judgments or not, I know how to clear them from my field.

For the five statements above, calculate your **FLOW #** _____

Judgments of any kind stop you from creating your future.

— KATHERINE MCINTOSH

___ I don't see color.
___ I see people just as people. I wish everyone would stop trying to suggest otherwise.
___ I let a thousand flowers bloom in my consciousness.
___ I am one with everyone.
___ I don't need a tool for clearing judgments.

For the five statements above, calculate your **GROW #** _____

Subtract your GROW # from your FLOW # to find out your KNOW # for Your Judgments.

FLOW - GROW = ______ KNOW

Congratulations to you for taking the time to know this aspect of yourself. You now know so much more about what you know and are open to what you don't know on this topic.

If your KNOW # is 17-25, your stream of consciousness on this topic is powerful.

If your KNOW # is 8-16, your stream of consciousness on this topic is steady but could be stronger if that's something you'd like.

If your KNOW # is from less than 0 to 7, your stream of consciousness on this topic is at a trickle.

What I've learned about Judgments

Thinking is difficult; that's why most people judge.

— CG JUNG

Over time, despite cooperating somewhat with their societally implanted judgments, my parents did encourage critical thinking and questioning of the existing order. I came to know more about most of my judgments on the basis of race, sex, or other criteria than I would have had I not consciously sought to eradicate them. But I didn't have any place to go from there. I wasn't aware of how many judgments I had about myself and others that I routinely made. And I had no idea that those judgments were constantly blocking my channel to my true inner guidance. So I certainly had no idea why or how to clear those judgments.

What I've learned may be controversial in the current era. Many think it's more important to know which judgments we have and where they came from than to eradicate them without knowing. I am a work in progress on this topic. It's helpful to know our history and understand where judgments have ripened into systemic bias. It's essential to recognize my own judgment and biases (and perhaps be less influenced by the judgments and biases of others, or at least to be more cautious in defending against them).

Humans are probably hardwired to judge to survive. Remember "remembering" earlier in this book? We examined it as a toxic mimic of knowing. Judgment itself may be a toxic mimic of knowing. To survive as a species, we had to figure out who, where, and what was dangerous and remember it for next time. This crucial evolutionary tactic worked well in past millennia but may impede the rapid evolution of our consciousness that is called for today.

As I write, we are in the middle of a huge transition in human consciousness. One of the reasons so many people are out in droves protesting is that both "sides" perceive change as an existential threat. It almost doesn't matter what that "change" is, whether it's the dissolution of binary male/female for life genders or whether it's the introduction of Christian Nationalism. Change itself is terrifying to the human animal.

Both "sides" are vestiges of an old model of consciousness. Judgment should not be conflated with *discernment* (a close cousin of *knowing*). Christian minister Terri Elton says, "discernment is a process for making decisions that draws on wisdom and requires opening oneself to outside sources." Notice the difference between *knowing* and *discernment* in this definition. The traditional Christian definition of discernment is basically to pray for guidance and then listen to your pastor and do what he says. Rev. Elton's meaning may be a little broader, but even in context, it leaves no room for listening to one's *inner* wisdom. God's voice is always outside of us in the traditional past. Never inside.

What is needed today is a new model of consciousness where judgments are recognized as barriers to human evolution and acknowledged and cleared in real time, allowing for what else is possible.

What can you do to strengthen your knowing of Judgments?

A tool to try: INTERESTING POINT OF VIEW — To clear judgments of others, say aloud, "Interesting point of view, I have that point of view" three times.

How, Why, Where & When to Use it: When you catch yourself judging others, say (under your breath if someone might hear) "interesting point of view: I have that point of view." Say it three times to really get it in your brain. This is another Access Consciousness tool. The concept is that every judgment we have of others is something that is inherently in us, not them. In essence, "interesting point of view, I have that point of view" means I replace *judgment* of the person I'm judging's actions and words with *curiosity* about their point of view. More than that, it means I experiment with owning the very point of view that I have been judging.

For example, I attend hot yoga several times a week at 6 am (yes, I'm trying to impress you with the hour I go, I'll own that). As I move my body in the early morning in (almost) 110-degree heat, I find my mind making space to judge much of what the instructor may be saying. If they are taking time out of my deep meditation and exercise to correct the movement or breathing of someone in the class, this has infuriated me. When I focus on what the instructor is or is not doing and whether they're doing it correctly, I'm effectively not in my body anymore, not in the yoga. I'm in judgment land.

It used to be that I had enough mindfulness to catch myself judging, but not enough to stop doing it. The best I could do was to change the channel in my mind, focusing on something else (and hey, don't knock changing the channel — that's a perfectly good hack, absent this one). Once I learned this tool, I started muttering, "interesting point of view," every time I noticed my mind judging. As I get curious about their point of view, the judgment (or barrier between us) melts. As I try owning that point of view, I notice that I'm judging my teacher for judging a student; I really am the same as my yoga teacher in that respect.

Using this tool melted away that judgment and brought me deeper into the yoga practice. It allowed me to giggle at myself instead of fuming at the teacher.

Affirmation

I CEASE RESISTING JUDGMENTS OR PRETENDING THEY'RE NOT THERE. INSTEAD, I APPROACH THEM WITH CURIOSITY, RECOGNIZING THAT EVERYTHING I'M JUDGING ABOUT SOMEONE ELSE IS SOMEHOW TRUE OF ME.

Reflection Questions

- What judgments keep popping up that I'm pretending are not there?
- What would it take for me to get curious about those?
- What would it take for me to own those judgments as judgments of me, too?
- Can I eliminate or change anything that doesn't allow me to see, know, be, and perceive?

CHAPTER 11

Know Your Food & Eating

Why you need to know your Food & Eating

More than ever, people are grasping the tremendous connection between food, eating habits, and health, as well as a life well-lived. Yet many of us know relatively little about what food or exercise serves us, including how to find that out and why. Some of us grew up being told *way* too much about nutrition and food as medicine. We learned to cook as children, and almost every meal was home-cooked, made from scratch. Some of us had busy parents who stocked the house with chips, soda, frozen food, or had a close relationship with a food delivery app. Some of us grew up with food insecurity, getting most of our meals at school or friends' homes, going to bed hungry often enough to remember it.

Do you know which foods and eating habits best serve you?

As adults, we have eaten what and how we learned to eat in childhood, whether it was what our parents fed us, or in reaction to parents who tried to control our food, or didn't or couldn't feed us well.

Some caregivers seemed to value a thin body more than they valued us or their health. Maybe they struggled with their weight or ours or both. The food they ate and the exercise they did would change constantly. This month, we're eating no carbs. Next, we're on smoothies only. Then, screw it, we're eating pizza and ice cream every minute of the day.

Regardless of how we were brought up, the question is how much we actually know about what foods serve us. Are we going by what society, our parents, and social media tell us, or do we *know* what we know about what is our right and perfect food, nutrition and way of eating?

Stream of Consciousness Inventory: Food & Eating

I have a regular food plan. I don't have to figure it out every day or week. To find out how powerful your food stream flows, rate each statement below on a scale of 1 to 5 according to how true/light that statement is for you. 5 indicates the statement is totally true/light, and 1 indicates that it is false/heavy. Add up your first five ratings to get your FLOW # and the second set of five ratings to get your GROW #. Subtract your GROW # from your FLOW # to get your current Food and Eating Stream of Consciousness Power.

Assign a number to each statement below on how true/light the statement feels for you, 5 being the most true.

___ I pay attention to what and how I eat. During some phases of my life, I've been able to eat certain foods and still feel healthy and fit. Other times, it seems I need to release certain foods and incorporate others.

___ I don't plan how I eat, but I'm naturally thin and healthy and can pretty much eat whatever I want.

___ I'm a "foodie," I love the way foods taste, smell, and are prepared. However, I've been shown that when a food is wrong for me, it doesn't taste or smell good to me, even if that's true for someone else.

___ Where I eat seems to matter. Restaurant-prepared food is too rich for me. I need to limit it to once or twice a month.

___ I make a "food and eating plan" regularly so I don't have to figure it out every day or week.

For the five statements above, calculate your **FLOW #** _____

Honestly, what's the point of trying to eat differently from how I do?

___ I eat foods that serve me, but I may not eat in a way that serves me. I eat fast, in front of devices, at my desk, in my car, without conscious enjoyment.

___ I grew up with certain foods that I eat and those are just the foods I continue to eat. I don't see the point of changing food.

___ I'm a "foodie." For me it's all about taste and the experience of eating. I could never give up any food if I like to eat it, whether or not it's "good for my body."

___ I eat three meals a day with one or two snacks and I eat most meals sitting down at a table with few distractions, but *what* I eat is not necessarily the best for me.

___ I'm too busy to establish any new routine, food, or exercise.

For the five statements above, calculate your **GROW #**_____

Subtract your GROW # from your FLOW # to find out your KNOW # for your Food & Eating.

FLOW - GROW = _______ KNOW

If your KNOW # is 17-25, congratulations, you know what food and exercise serve you. You might be a *Super Streamer of* Food & Eating.

If your KNOW # is 8-16, you have some confidence in your ability to know your Food & Eating, but maybe you could use some help trusting yourself more.

If your KNOW # is from less than 0 to 7, it could be an indication that you are alienated from your body and soul's wisdom about Food & Eating.

What I've learned about Food & Eating

My story with food starts before consistent memories, but here's what seems to have happened: When I was two and a half, my 2-month-old baby brother Phillip died of what is now known as Sudden Infant Death Syndrome. Soon after that, a doctor diagnosed me with "failure to thrive," so it ceased being an option for me to turn down food. By the time I hit kindergarten, I was alive and well but overweight and a compulsive overeater. I was sad and teased at school, so the solution was to get me to lose weight. Our mother toggled between trying to get me to eat and trying to get me not to eat. We had lots of snacks, unclear meal times, and late dinners at which there was no option not to eat, no matter how many snacks I consumed to get to dinner.

You guessed it; this produced a lifetime of compulsive eating and dieting. I was a champion weight loser, usually losing the most weight that the diet claimed was possible to lose in a given period of time. And then I'd be at goal weight for about a minute and a half, only to gain it all back with interest. I fluctuated between a large and an extra-large size in high school. In college, I was between extra large and 2XL, and in graduate school and early motherhood, I got up to 3 or 4XL, topping out at 90 pounds over a healthy weight.

I wouldn't try any diet that required me to weigh and measure my food or eat a "balanced" plate with one serving of protein, one serving of carbohydrate, and one serving of vegetables. I couldn't commit to a real meal time, or give up snacking between meals, or even admit there were any times where I shouldn't eat.

I preferred diets that weren't remotely like anything someone could eat for life, ones with zero carbohydrates, or ones where you could have nothing but cabbage.

Eating no carbohydrates really worked for me for a while. For years, I subsisted on virtually nothing but hamburger, lettuce, and mayonnaise. At the onset of middle age, it stopped working. The weight started to come back on despite my weird plan (and I was getting physically ill from it). I was panicking. I just couldn't do this again. The lettuce burger mayo diet worked. It wasn't really even a diet anymore. It was how I ate.

At about the same time, some business partners and I sought outside coaching. The business failed, but the coaching was a success, and it led me into a 12-step program for compulsive eating. I also accompanied our young son Nick with a long-term illness to a series of health providers (as described in Chapter "Know Your Body & Healing"). It took years for him to find the proper cure, but early on, Dr. Michael Kwiker, an osteopath in Sacramento, introduced me to the possibility of learning more about what food and sustainable eating practices really served me.

By putting Nick on the O-Blood type diet,[14] this doctor changed both of our lives. To support Nick, and because it was called a "diet," I also followed the O blood type diet. It seemed perfect for me. It was similar to zero-carbohydrate or paleo plans, as I had long adhered to, but with some differences. In two weeks of eating that way, Nick's extreme intestinal symptoms had disappeared, while my whole system seemed to have backed up. I had extreme constipation, cramping, abdominal pain and low energy.

It turned out that, contrary to my own belief, I was *not* an O blood type. I am an A blood type. When I switched to the A plan, everything began to change. As long as I ate the "beneficial" foods and avoided the "poison" foods, my weight fell off. My digestion has improved beyond what I ever thought possible. I experienced no more sinus headaches or infections, and I had fewer cravings. I still needed to manage my lifelong addiction to compulsive eating, but I now knew what foods really served me.

People can also have different eating habits that serve them well. Some people benefit most from three meals a day with nothing in between. Some people feel healthiest when they eat multiple small meals. Some people's bodies really respond to "intermittent fasting," which involves confining your meals to certain hours, often with most hours *not* eating.

Now, let me be clear: even though both clients changed my life, I'm not here to sell you on a 12-step approach or a particular way of eating. The point of every section of this book is to guide you to

14 *Eat Right 4 Your Type* by Dr. Peter J. D'Adamo

your own internal *knowing*, not mine. I firmly believe that food can be both medicine and poison, and that to get well, we need to know which foods serve us and which don't. However, I also believe that we are the ones who know best which foods (and ways of eating) work for us and which ones don't. *You* are the one who needs to listen to *you*. What can you do to strengthen your *knowing* of Food & Eating?

What can you do to know your Food & Eating?

A tool to try: CANDLE FLAME — What effect does a food or eating choice have on your internal candle flame?

How, Why, Where & When to Use it: Picture a candle burning bright in your chest. Now, if you avoid a particular food or try a specific food plan, what happens to the candle? If you take the contrary action, what happens to the candle? Generally, if the candle burns brighter and stronger, that's a yes; if it burns weaker and flickers or goes out, that's a no.

As with all tools, consider trying the tool several times before deciding whether it's right for you. The Light vs. Heavy tool didn't work for me for a while because I was focusing on the wrong things. Some people report that they can't "picture" something. If that's you, this tool may not be for you. The *Is it Light for Me Tool* works by feeling energy, not picturing something, so that tool may work better for you.

Affirmation

I KNOW WHICH FOODS AND WAYS OF EATING
SERVE ME AND WHICH DON'T.
I AM AT PEACE WITH MY FOOD AND EATING.

Reflection Questions

- What are you being shown is most true for you with Food & Eating?
- Is there something you're being led to change?
- What tool that you've heard about in this section or another do you think would be most likely to help you move forward?
- What's one small step you're willing to take, and by when will you do it?

CHAPTER 12

Know Your Love & Sex Life

I'd never join a club that would allow a person like me to become a member.

— GROUCHO MARX

Why you need to know your love & sex life

While there are myriad books, websites, and dating apps on how to attract and retain a partner, there's an assumption built into those products that a) the most crucial quality in a partner is compatibility: b) the more alike you are, the more "compatible" you'll be; so almost no emphasis is put on your own inner knowing of whether it serves you to be in a sex or love relationship, what type of relationship that would or could be, or what type of person best meets your needs.

A woman who once used one of the *know* tools on the fly with me during a talk realized in under two minutes that the reason she didn't have a partner is because she didn't *want* one. It was that simple. I'll explain later in this section how to use the tool of "havingness" to get that inner knowing.

The point is that we can blunder along with sex and love, looking for something we may or may not want, while all the while *not* asking for something we actually *do* want.

In this section, we can assess where we are and what we know about our relationship with sex and with love (and maybe the relationship *between* sex and love). How important is sex to us? How important is love? Where are we in harmony? Where are we in discord? Like that.

Stream of Consciousness Inventory: Love & Sex Life

The best relationships are a balance of connection and freedom.

— ESTHER PEREL

To find out how powerful your Love & Sex Life stream flows, rate each statement below on a scale of 1 to 5 according to how true/light that statement is for you. 5 indicates the statement is totally true/light, and 1 indicates that it is false/heavy. Add up your first five ratings to get your FLOW # and the second set of five ratings to get your GROW #. Subtract your GROW # from your FLOW # to get your current Love & Sex Life Stream Power.

Assign a number to each statement below on how true/light the statement feels for you, 5 being the most true.

___ I can be attracted to someone without falling in love overnight, and I can fall in love without obsessing

___ I do not have to control the ones I love nor let them control me.

___ I love myself as much as I love others.

___ I ask my partner for what I need.
___ I am present in body, mind, and spirit during sex.

For the five statements above, calculate your **FLOW #** _____

___ I feel lost or uprooted without a partner.
___ Having few healthy boundaries, I become emotionally attached and/or sexually involved with people without knowing them.
___ Fearing emotional and/or sexual deprivation, I compulsively pursue and involve myself in one relationship after another, sometimes having more than one sexual or emotional liaison at a time.
___ I sexualize stress, guilt, loneliness, anger, shame, fear, and envy. I use sex or emotional dependence as substitutes for nurturing care and support.
___ I use sex and emotional involvement to manipulate and control others.

For the five statements above, calculate your **GROW #** _____

Subtract your GROW # from your FLOW # to find out your KNOW # for your Love & Sex Life.

FLOW - GROW = _______ KNOW

If your KNOW # is 17-25, congratulations, you're aware that your partner is not your source, you love yourself, and to some extent, you are aware and able to articulate your needs. You just might be a *Super Streamer* of Love & Sex Life.

If your KNOW # is 8-16, you have experiences of being in love with yourself, but also have used love and sex for other purposes.

If your KNOW # is from less than 0 to 7, it could be an indication that getting, protecting and having sex or love rules your life.

What I've learned about Love & Sex

As a young child, I was teased at school, picked last for sports teams, and left out of birthday parties and other events. I retreated into fantasy. I read many books and stories about magic and princesses. And I had strong crushes on multiple boys. As I moved into adolescence, the crushes got stronger. It was basically all I could talk about with friends. I would think and scheme and plot about boys, but, like the Groucho Marx quote above, my rejection of myself was so extreme that throughout high school, I didn't want to date boys who liked me.

This continued into my first year of college, which, to my horror, I entered as a virgin (primarily because of this Groucho Marxist policy above). After lowering myself to chase unavailable men during my freshman year, I finally fell mutually in love with a man for the first time. However, part of what allowed me to make the shift was that for various reasons, we chose to communicate and meet in secret. This was so exciting and fun that it made up for the fact that we actually liked each other!

This secret affair was so exhilarating that I developed a taste for the adrenaline of secrecy. That cycle of secrecy and excitement with love and sex continued until I met the man who would become my husband and came to grips with the pain that pattern could cause not only others but myself. It turned out that the experience of hiding and cheating reinforced a childhood pattern of not asking for what

I needed. As I stopped seeking emotional validation outside my primary relationship, I was compelled to get to know myself and ask for what I needed.

People I've counseled have experienced different patterns with love and sex, many dysfunctional enough to be labeled sex or love addiction.[15] Many women continue my early pattern of being overly attracted to emotionally unavailable people well into adulthood, so much so that they can be termed a "love addict." The people they are attracted to can sometimes be termed "love avoidants." This kind of relationship can settle into a cycle whereby the love avoidant pulls away from any real intimacy until they sense their love addict is losing interest. At that point, they become charming and reel the love addict back in.[16]

Some have suffered from what can be known as sexual or emotional anorexia, whereby they withdraw from almost all social situations and live lives of isolation. Some have coupled anorexia and isolation with addiction to porn or paid sex.[17]

Some have simply been serial adulterers, a pattern once expected and celebrated in men and scorned in women. Many of these individuals end up getting married and divorced multiple times. Each time they get married, they swear off cheating. And then they do it again.

Even those in "normal" non-addictive relationships often know they want more from the relationship than they are receiving. In these instances, they may yearn for greater emotional and/or sexual intimacy with their partner without communicating their needs. Many

---

15 *Sex and Love Addicts Anonymous: The Basic Text* for *The Augustine Fellowship* by Sex and Love Addicts Anonymous

16 *Facing Love Addiction* by Pia Mellody

17 *Out of the Shadows: Understanding Sex Addiction* by Patrick Carnes

people, especially women, find it hard to know what they know and express their needs to their partners. There are additional tools for improving knowing in the Appendix section on Clearing the Way for Knowing for better communication, and also just shifting their own consciousness.

One easy tool that both increases *knowing* and can instantly shift consciousness so we receive what we know we want is the Havingness tool:

What can you do to know your Love & Sex?

A tool to try: THE HAVINGNESS GAUGE

It's one thing to *want* and another entirely to *have*. We can "want" all kinds of things, but whether we actually "have" them depends on the degree to which we are willing to have them. The *havingness gauge* is a way to measure how much we're ready and willing to receive that which we say we desire. And when we see that and *know what we know* about our *havingness*, then we can either actually *have* it, or, perhaps, realize that we really weren't up for having it and move on.

In your mind's eye, picture a sort of gas gauge like on the dashboard of a car with 100% on the left and 0% on the right. That's the "havingness gauge."[18]

Think of something that you think you already want. Since this is a section on sex and love, maybe that's a life partner, or better sex, or a better relationship with your current partner. Or perhaps it's just a sense of contentment with having no partner at all.

Whatever it is, look at the gauge and see where the needle goes when you think of actually *having* that which you say you want. As with all *know* tools, don't overthink it. Let's say that you want a life partner, and when you picture the gauge, the havingness needle springs to 25%. That means you are only 25% willing to receive what you claim to desire.

Now, picture the needle moving from 25% to 100% instantly, just swooshing over from left to right, as if your "havingness" tank is filled to the brim. What, if anything, do you notice is being released or happening to move from 25% to 100% havingness? Make note of that if you can.

Some people almost instantly receive what they want just by forcing the needle to 100%. Some people sense a release of stuck energy from wherever it was—and that moves the "havingness" needle. Some people actually perceive specific beliefs or thoughts leaving the field and allowing the needle to move. And *some* people, like the woman I mentioned at the beginning of this section, just instantly realize, "Oh, this is not something I am willing to have or want to have. I've just been pretending I want it."

18 A tool gleaned from the Berkeley Psychic Institute

Affirmation

I AM WORTHY OF THE LOVE AND SEX LIFE I WISH TO HAVE.
I ASK FOR WHAT I NEED AND I RECEIVE IT.

Reflection Questions

- Now that I know more about my love and sex life, what does that suggest?
- What changes might I want to make?
- What's my degree of "havingness" for what I say I want?
- What do I need to release to "have" it?

CHAPTER 13

Know Your Money & Finances

Is it finally time to take over the steering wheel and find out who and what you truly be with money?[19]

— DR. DAIN HEER

The Importance of knowing your money & finances

We all engage with money and finances. Many of us think of money as a finite resource that limits and determines our choices in life. We have X amount of money; therefore, we can do some things and not others. And while there's a way that this is true, the energy of money is one more "reality" that may be driven by our choices, thoughts, beliefs, and opinions, rather than our choices being driven by the "reality" (read: scarcity) of money.[20]

There are numerous resources available on how to manage and track finances. There's also plenty of encouragement and advice on how to accumulate, consolidate, or reduce debt. Many preach "prosperity" consciousness, or the "law of attraction," both of which can veer into

---

19 Dr. Dain Heer, Access Consciousness

20 *Busting Loose from the Money Game* by Robert Scheinfeld

magical thinking and trap us in polarities between poverty and wealth.

But how many people are encouraging us to dial into our own inner knowing about money? How many are asking us to inventory our thoughts, beliefs, opinions, and conclusions about finances? Here, we take a look at those thoughts and focus on how to get out of vagueness and magical thinking with money by really seeing how we are and what we know.

Stream of Consciousness Inventory: Money & Finances

It's right there on the dollar bill, "In God We Trust"[21]

To find out how powerful your Money & Finances stream flows, rate each statement below on a scale of 1 to 5 according to how true/light that statement is for you. 5 indicates the statement is totally true/light, and 1 indicates that it is false/heavy. Add up your first five ratings to get your FLOW # and the second set of five ratings to get your GROW #. Subtract your GROW # from your FLOW # to get your current Money & Finances Stream Power.

Assign a number to each statement below on how true/light the statement feels for you, 5 being the most true.

___ I make choices based on what feels most substantial for me, not how much money I have.
___ I know when expenses come due and how much they'll be.
___ I know that the Universe is my source, not my employer, spouse, parent, or something else.

21 Sandy Beach

___ I am in the flow of money—it comes through me and goes out to create in the world.

___ I keep track of my money carefully and know where it is and where it goes.

For the five statements above, calculate your **FLOW #** _____

Money was dope, money was extra food, money was... vagueness.[22]

___ Some have money and some people don't. I wasn't born rich, so I'll never be or feel rich.

___ I am unclear about my financial situation: I don't know my account balances, monthly expenses, loan interest rates, fees, fines, or contractual obligations.

___ I don't plan for taxes, retirement, or other not-recurring but predictable items and then I feel surprised when they come due.

___ I live in chaos and drama around money: using one credit card to pay another, bouncing checks, always having a financial crisis to contend with.

___ I have unwarranted inhibition and embarrassment in what could be normal discussions of money.

For the five statements above, calculate your **GROW #** _____

22 Debtors Anonymous

Subtract your GROW # from your FLOW # to find out your KNOW # for your Money & Finances

FLOW - GROW = _______ KNOW

If your KNOW # is 17-25, congratulations, you're aware that money is not your source, but you respect money and keep track of it. You just might be a *Super Streamer* of Money & Finances.

If your KNOW # is 8-16, you have experiences of being in the flow of money, but also fear and constriction.

If your KNOW # is from less than 0 to 7, it could be an indication that getting, protecting, and having money rules your life, and maybe you hate and fear money and having to manage it.

What I've learned about Money & Finance

I've never really been broke or been afraid of where I'd sleep or how I'd eat. I grew up in a comfortably middle-class home where one side of the family considered it gauche to discuss money and the other liked to. I married into the same thing. Yet, my relationship with money, similar to my relationships with food and eating, and people and work, brought me to my knees a few years ago.

What Happens in Vagueness Stays in Vagueness

When a friend said to me, "What happens in vagueness stays in vagueness." I laughed and said, "Well if *vagueness* is a standard for having a problem with money, then sign me up. I probably made (I pause for a quick calculation) $1200 worth of mistakes last month alone." I had in mind everything from paying late fees to buying airfare too late.

She said, "I could live on your mistakes." It was like the universe punched me in the stomach. I doubled over with the realization that I was squandering the universe's resources, not respecting the energy of money and what it can buy and do.

As I stayed up all night that evening thinking about myself and money, I realized further that although I was posing as an adult, my disrespect for money revealed otherwise. In my marriage, I was a full and equal partner in child-rearing, housework, cooking, vacation planning (basically everything but money). I had made it through 25 years of joint finances without knowing:

- What accounts we had
- How much was in those accounts
- How to access them
- When annual recurring expenses came due (like vehicle renewal, property taxes, subscriptions, etc.)
- When credit cards were due
- How we paid them off every month
- How much money we had coming in every month
- How much money we had going out

Obviously, it takes a certain amount of privilege, support and resources to be able to pull off this level of vagueness without eventually living in your car. (Note: Not that it requires vagueness to live in your car—these days in my region, many people without extra resources or support end up living on the street.) But I realized I had always lived in a state of vagueness around money. Even though I started babysitting at 12 (just because I wanted to), I never really had kept track of anything that well. It was always random.

Then, after I hit bottom in late middle age, with the help of others whose financial struggles and overspending had led them deep into real debt and jeopardy, I began to track my own expenditures.

Side note: I've learned that many people who do not perceive themselves to be wealthy or abundant believe that the goal of wealth is not to have to think about or keep track of money. As someone who is now wealthy by any world standard, but has not always strictly been so, I'd observe that that's both true and not true. It's true, in that I can no longer blame money for why I'm not doing something I say I want to do. It's not true, in that almost anyone who is rich and stays rich watches not only their dollars but their pennies.

Case in point: Years ago, I was a consumer lobbyist working in coalition with discount stores and their founders. These guys would come to Washington, D.C., to lobby Congress with me and their lobbyist. Yet when these millionaires went to lunch in the Senate cafeteria, they'd literally haggle over the price of a scoop of cottage cheese, and it would usually be one of their lawyers (who are workers, not owners of the means of production) who would pick up the tab. It was hilarious and mind-boggling to watch them in action.

It didn't make sense to me until I later read some book about the habits of millionaires, which showed that, sure enough, it is a common trait of those with many millions of dollars to keep track of their pennies.

Despite observing that truth years before, here I was, years later, a middle-aged adult keeping track of my pennies for the first time ever. My money mentors advised me to keep every receipt and write down every expenditure not, as I would have previously tried to do it, by putting all the receipts in a giant bag and going through them months later, but by staying on top of it day by day.

They told me to keep track of my expenses for three months and then to get together with two other people to have them go over my "books." They even suggested that my husband attend that meeting. That suggestion terrified me. "That's never going to happen," I swore. "He'll never let some random strangers look at our finances."

Well, a few months later, that's exactly what happened. My partner and I sat down with two other people that he had never met and I barely knew, and they looked over our "numbers," as they called them. Who knew that having another pair of eyes on your money was so valuable? Their suggestions changed my life.

Before that, I was not only vague about my own finances, but I was also vague about my business. Actually, I knew the finances of the organization I ran to the penny. The problem wasn't that. It was that I was co-dependently failing to pay the most important employee (me!). That all had to be changed before I could even get into my home finances. Month after month, with the small non-profit I ran, we'd reach the end of the month and there wouldn't be enough money left over to pay myself. Since my husband had a steady paycheck and we had enough money, I would just pay all the organization's other bills first and not my own salary.

After my first pressure relief group, I became willing to pay the most important employee first, not last.

What can you do to know your Money & Finance?

A tool to try: THE DOUBLE-BLIND PAPER TEST — Many people feel money drives choices. Some assert choices drive money. When we understand what we know, we can move beyond vagueness and act in alignment with the flow of money. This can support our choosing according to what's light and joyful rather than by what we think we can afford.

One of the many ways to *know what you know*, and this is a great tool for skeptics, is this Double-Blind Paper Test to discern light or heavy for multiple competing choices.

Why Use it: You have multiple competing possibilities for your time, and you are stuck in your head about it and can't trust yourself enough to compare each one without putting your finger on the scale of your consciousness.

How to Use it: Say I've budgeted for a one-week trip to an exotic world destination and I'm trying to decide between four possible locations. Cut four pieces of paper to be exactly the same shape and size. Write each destination on one side, turn them over, mix them around, and then on the other side write "1," "2," "3," "4." (It doesn't matter which one has which number, and doesn't have to be a number; It could be a letter or an animal sticker or a color. Just don't overthink it and *don't* make note of which destination has which number on the other side!)

With the destinations facing down, move them all around so that there's no particular order to them. Then put your hand over each piece of paper and feel whether it feels light or heavy (or, if you prefer, whether the flame burns brighter or flickers and threatens to go out). In a separate notebook or Apple Note, write down on a scale of 1 to 5 how light it feels, with 5 being the lightest or perhaps the brightest flame. As you see the code in your notebook, again feel into it and make a note of it.

Determine which of all the options is the lightest. Note that you are now double or maybe triple blind on this, so that it's not just about your conscious mind making the decision.

Turn over the papers and see which option felt the most expansive for you without your knowing how expensive it is. Do the entire test again with different papers if you feel that the test was unfair, and see whether the results are the same.

Affirmation

I KNOW HOW MUCH THINGS COST AND WHAT MY CURRENT EXPENSES ARE.

Reflection Questions

- What keeps you from choosing from a place of joy and lightness rather than lack and insecurity?
- How can clarity support knowing what you know?
- What if you did not perceive that your choices were constrained by money? (But without credit card debt)

CHAPTER 14

Know Your Stuff

Intimate, necessary details add up to one's private life. Select them with care because they are your life.

— ALEXANDRA STODDARD

Why you need to know your stuff

Why *would* you want to know your stuff? We all have stuff; we're talking physical stuff: books, clothes, furniture, souvenirs, gifts we never use, gifts we never gave. Stuff. And for those of us who came of age before the internet, much of the stuff that is now digitized and on the cloud for everyone else is in physical reality for us: paperback books, paper files, CDs, DVDs, even LPs and VHS, and the machines and shelves that read and play and hold all that stuff. The older we are, the more stuff we probably have because we've had more time to accumulate it and, as we just covered, less of it is stored digitally.

So the stuff is there, but what do we know about ourselves in relation to it? Do we pretend it's not here? Are we super organized with it? Are we a minimalist to the point of never having anything?

Does it weigh on us? Are we careful or careless with it? Like that…

Let's find out.

Stream of Consciousness Inventory: Your Stuff

Clutter is not just physical stuff, it's old ideas, toxic relationships and bad habits.

— ELEANOR BROWN

To find out how powerfully your Stuff stream flows, rate each statement below on a scale of 1 to 5 according to how true/light that statement is for you. 5 indicates the statement is totally true/light, and 1 indicates that it is false/heavy. Add up your first five ratings to get your FLOW # and the second set of five ratings to get your GROW #. Subtract your GROW # from your FLOW # to get your current Stuff Stream Power.

Assign a number to each statement below based on how true/light the statement feels for you, with 5 being the most true.

___ I have a place for everything and everything in its place.

___ Every object in my home, whether it is displayed or packed away, is important to me because it reminds me of a person or a time in my life.

___ I don't care about possessions much. I hardly see or notice them.

___ I don't organize my stuff or pay a lot of attention to it, but I notice that when I'm in someone else's well-organized space it feels better to me than my own rather chaotic environment.

___ I just want to be able to get a hold of the things I need quickly and easily.

For the five statements above, calculate your **FLOW #** _____

Get rid of clutter and you may just find that it was blocking the door you've been looking for.

— KATRINA MAYER

___ I love the idea of systems and creating them, but I don't consistently use them.

___ I periodically go scorched earth with stuff. I go through huge piles over the course of hours, creating categories and moving much of it out of the house.

___ I don't have an issue with my stuff but other people's cluttered homes drive me crazy.

___ Look, lots of physical stuff in a home is only an issue if it's an issue. I have tons of stuff all over the place, and it's not an issue or a priority.

___ I don't need and don't have systems for stuff. I am fine with not very much stuff.

For the five statements above, calculate your **GROW #** _____

Subtract your GROW # from your FLOW # to find out your KNOW # for Your Stuff.

FLOW - GROW = _______ KNOW

Congratulations to you for taking the time to know this aspect of yourself. You now know so much more about what you know and what you don't know about Stuff.

If your KNOW # is 17-25, your stream of consciousness on the topic of Stuff has a powerful flow.

If your KNOW # is 8-16, your stream of consciousness on this topic is steady but could be stronger if that's something you'd like.

If your KNOW # is from less than 0 to 7, your stream of consciousness on this topic is at a trickle.

What I've learned about Stuff

However your mind is, that's how your home will be.
If you free your mind of clutter, your home
will be uncluttered.

— SISTER SHIVANI

I had really thought it was the other way around, that I had to clear clutter to have a clear mind, but that's not how it turned out. Years ago, I took a workshop on spirituality and clutter. I took it for my mother, not me. My mother had a problem with stuff. Not me. You guessed it, I learned in that class that it wasn't my mother who had a problem with stuff, it was me. She was fine with it. She loved her things, her pervasive clutter. And she was not interested in letting go of basically any of it, except maybe papers and certain piles that she had earmarked for giveaway (perish the thought of throwing an object in the trash).

I learned that I was the one with a problem with stuff because a) I was preoccupied with *her* stuff, and that *she* needed to do something about it and give it away. And b) I really didn't stay on top of my own stuff all that well. Maybe I could actually focus on my own stuff instead of hers if I thought good stuff management was so important.

The teacher gave us a personality test about our attitude towards clutter (or stuff), in which I learned that I was a type that is attracted to systems, has good intentions, but then doesn't use the systems that are set up. As a result, I never have or follow any consistent protocol with any of my stuff. I leave my laundry, clean or dirty, all over the floor. I have drawers and places for it, but if I use them, I shove it in there instead of folding, etc., and then I periodically go on this big tear where I sort through all of it at once and give away vast amounts of it and create a new "system" and then swear to use it. And then I don't. And I'm that way with every part of stuff, not just laundry, but files, books, food; you name it. I think she suggested that I periodically create a system, but make the "system" as simple as possible so that I might have a chance of using it. And then schedule a quarterly reboot for looking at the "system" (which motivates me) rather than dealing with the stuff (which does not).

Ever since finding out that I'm a person who can't really maintain a clutter system, I stopped trying to find "systems" for that. Something about that *knowing* (and clearing of judgment around that) allowed me to just relax and allow myself to just be the way I am. Since that time, strangely, without effort, our home has become less and less cluttered and clearer, making it more enjoyable for me to live in. What Sister Shivani says has proven to be true. The less cluttered my mind, the less cluttered my environment.

However, the converse is also true: the less cluttered my home, the less cluttered my mind. As I started decluttering my mind (particularly of judgments of myself and others), I found myself naturally clearing areas of the home that had gone unattended so long I didn't even see the clutter anymore. The more you know about *you* and your relationship to stuff, the more you can actually tailor your own system (or lack thereof) to what works for you. It's also entirely possible, and to a certain extent, this is true of me, that what you'll learn is that managing stuff or being the person who keeps a tidy house is never going to be for you. If so, maybe just coming to peace with that is your knowing and journey. Actually, stop beating yourself up and expecting it to be otherwise.

What can you do to know your Stuff?

A tool to try: WHAT ELSE IS POSSIBLE?[23] — Ask aloud the question, "What else is possible?" and allow yourself to receive help from your Higher Self. This will stir up new possibilities where you currently don't see any good choices.

How to Use it with Stuff: Whether you're actively seeking to get rid of stuff, changing your relationship with it, or wanting to stop judging yourself and others around *their* acquisition, display, and retention of "stuff," you can ask aloud, "What else is possible?" (You can whisper it or say it under your breath if you feel embarrassed, but saying it aloud actually goes over really well too in *most* circumstances.)

Why, Where & When to Use it: Anytime you're feeling stuck or like there are no good options is the time to use this tool. That can be profound existential crises or despair, which I've seen occur when people are facing mountains of stuff, whether it be their own or their loved ones stuff. Or it can be in mundane situations like just going through your closet during a season change and trying to figure out what to get rid of and what to keep. You can also always turn to the Light vs. Heavy tool here. Is this piece of clothing light for me or heavy (energetically)? This is similar to Marie Kondo's question: Does this

---

23 Access Consciousness tool – www.accessconsciousness.com

bring me joy? Just asking this question aloud shifts me from being only interested in what I think are the parameters of the possible to accessing the part of me that is connected to the unlimited. And then, having said it, your only job is to get curious and pay attention to what thoughts, signs, and occurrences happen that may bring a "new" thought, or possibility to your consciousness.

With stuff, maybe I can't figure out where or how to get rid of something, either emotionally or physically. In using this tool, some people decide that "what else is possible?" is an internet research project. While some research may not be harmful, it's not the point of this question. The question is there to get us out of the known, stuck, limited old thoughts we have, and to get us *curious* about other possibilities. Curious is not the same as, "I have to figure this out now." Curious is more like the energy of:

> "Oh, there are other possibilities here than I'm seeing," (like that's just a fact).
> "I wonder what they are? I'd better pay attention!"
> "How fun it is to pay attention and know that something cool and new (that maybe saves my life) is going to show up!"

You never know what ideas or even amazing coincidences will occur. A neighbor stops by and falls in love with all 25 boxes of things you have. Or better yet, begs you to let her be the person who combs through your mother's belongings after she's died.

In my case, when we were cleaning our family home for sale, I suddenly discovered a company that comes to the house, cleans out house and the yard completely, puts everything that looks important or like it could be of high sentimental or financial value in one room, bags up all the trash, puts everything else that could potentially be sold in another room. Now that it's all cleaned up, they let you go through everything and decide what you want to keep. THEN they do an estate sale. And then takes everything that didn't sell away. THEN, get this, they actually put the house on the market as real estate agents, stage and run all that. All costs associated with cleaning, etc., are forgiven if you list the house. I never dreamed such a company could exist. It was a fantastic find–truly an answer to what else is possible for me.

Affirmation

As I unclutter my mind, I unclutter my home.
As I unclutter my home, I unclutter my mind.

Reflection Questions

- How can I declutter my mind to unclutter my home?
- How can I declutter my home to unclutter my mind?
- Where am I judging myself or others unnecessarily regarding stuff?
- What else is possible?

CHAPTER 15

Know Your Time

For your life to be harmonious, you need to develop a harmonious relationship with time.

— GAY HENDRICKS[24]

Why Knowing Time is Important

How are you with time? Do you know? Do you pay attention? Most of us have a relationship with time, even if we aren't fully aware of what it is. Habitually, we may be extremely or a little bit late, or downright early. We may schedule every aspect of our lives. We may only schedule key events and let everything else fall into place. We may have a clear idea of how many hours a week it takes us to do all the things we do, such as shopping, cooking, eating, dressing, sleeping, exercising, or relaxing. Or we may have no clue, or, most likely, be somewhere in between on all of this.

Most of us believe time is limited. Some of us behave as if that's true. Others behave as if it's not. Almost regardless of our beliefs, some of us resent time bitterly. We want to do absolutely everything,

24 Hendricks, Gay, *The Big Leap: Conquer Your Hidden Fear and Take Life to the Next Level*

and there never seems to be enough of it. We approach it the way some approach money, feeling it is a scarce resource that prevents happiness or choice.

So it's useful to get clear on both the Minerva (stressed, left brain, linear) version of time (the thoughts, beliefs, options and conclusions we have about it) and the Nirvana (relaxed, right brain, expansive) version, what our unlimited Higher Self knows is true. Like most of these segments, I've had experience with both the scarcity and anger at the apparent limitation of time, and a change and feeling of spaciousness. I've also, like with most areas of life, had an opportunity to fake it until I make it. All of this and more is available as you read on.

Stream of Consciousness Inventory: Time

Time you enjoy wasting is not wasted time.

— MARTHE TROLY-CURTIN[25]

To find out how powerful Time stream flows, rate each statement below on a scale of 1 to 5 according to how true/light that statement is for you. 5 indicates the statement is totally true/light, and one indicates that it is false/heavy. Add up your first five ratings to get your FLOW # and the second set of five ratings to get your GROW #. Subtract your GROW # from your FLOW # to get your Time Stream Power.

Assign a number to each statement below on how true/light the statement feels for you, 5 being the most true.

25 from *Phrynette Married*

___ Even when I'm hard at work, I notice what I'm feeling emotionally or physically.
___ When I'm doing something I love, I notice that time stands still.
___ I trust that there will be enough time.
___ I value joy over efficiency.
___ I am where time comes from.

For the five statements above, calculate your **FLOW #** _____

It's not enough to be busy, so are the ants.
The question is, what are we busy about?[26]

___ I run perpetually late and feel bad about it.
___ I blame lack of time for why I can't do what I want to do.
___ I either feel rushed (not enough time) or bored (too much of it).
___ I do not have time to do the creative thinking that would make the biggest difference in my life.
___ Other people have time for lots of things, but not me.

For the five statements above, calculate your **GROW #** _____

Subtract your GROW # from your FLOW # to find out your KNOW # for Time

FLOW - GROW = _______ KNOW

26 Harry David Thoreau

Congratulations to you for taking the time to know this aspect of yourself. You now know so much more about what you know and what you don't know about Time.

If your KNOW # is 17-25, your stream of consciousness on Time has a powerful flow.

If your KNOW # is 8-16, your stream of consciousness on Time is steady but could be stronger if that's something you'd like.

If your KNOW # is from less than less than 0 to 7, your stream of consciousness on Time is at a trickle.

What I've learned about Time

You're where time comes from.

— GAY HENDRICKS

Like everything in this book. It's not important that you change or adopt my perspective on time use (but I do have one). What's important is learning more about what *you* know about time. I hope that hearing some of my journey with time will inspire you to imagine what else is possible with you and time.

Time has had its way with me. Our mother ran perpetually, hilariously, perilously late. She kept clocks and watches set 15 to 30 minutes early to increase her chances of a timely arrival. Later in her life, my brother once created a photo collage of all the clocks in her house, taken at roughly the same moment. Every single clock showed a radically different time. In a way, that's how we all are. Each of us has a radically different relationship with time.

You'd think this upbringing would have me arriving early or on the dot, but you'd be wrong. Part of my way of coping with my upbringing was to keep busy and schedule myself tightly every day and for everything. To keep myself safe, my young self concluded it had to ...

> Get out of the house.
> Get to a class.
> Get to a rehearsal.
> Get to a party.
> Avoid idle gaps.
> Leave no room for incursions or doubt.
> And be sue to leave no room for the "failure" that I ascribed to my mother.

This strategy continued well into adulthood so that I typically arrived 10-15 minutes late unless it was "really important," in which case I arrived on the dot or one or two minutes late. It wasn't until I took a coaching class[27] for my business that my relationship with time began to change. I committed to being in my seat on time, but I wasn't "on time" by their standards and spent a couple of hours having everyone in the class watch me be "coached" on why I didn't keep my commitments. I emerged from this experience with my timepieces kept on the actual time going forward and a new goal of arriving early so that I can really be on time. This marked the beginning of a long journey to understanding what I know about time.

I needed to stop blaming time and take full responsibility for my choices

Gay Hendricks' description of *Einstein Time*[28] was life-changing for me. He challenged readers to go on what he called a "time diet"–

27 Mastering Life's Energies at the Academy for Coaching Excellence

28 *The Big Leap* by Gay Hendricks

ceasing to blame time for anything you did or didn't want to do. Hendricks points out that many people blame time as a reason not to do something because they think it's kinder than just admitting the truth. The people around us can argue with whether there's really enough time, but they can't argue with our preferences.

By this point, we were at the part of my mother's life where I was dropping her off, not the other way around. Because mom never wanted our visits to end, I would typically say, "Sorry, I don't have time" (to do whatever else she wanted to do). Hendricks taught me that this was a lie. I *did* have time; I just chose to do something else with it. This is always the case. There is (at least the appearance of) time, and we are constantly *choosing* how to "spend" it. So I started experimenting with saying, instead, "Sorry, Mom. That's not how I want to spend the rest of the day. I have other things I want to do." And, BAM! Just like that, no argument from her at all. I had learned that there's such a thing as an inarguable statement, and nothing's more inarguable than stating a preference or making a choice.

The concept of "Einstein Time" is another aspect of a Nirvana, rather than a Minerva way of approaching life. For real, quantum physicists have proven that everything we call time is actually fictional. Wrap your mind around this if you can: Particle physicists have observed the exact same quantum Particle (not similar, same) being in different places at the exact same time. There is no time at the level of the quantum field or "ground of all being."

That means that, quite literally, we are the generators of time in our lives (just as we generate money and purpose and everything else). Ceasing blaming time for what I do or want to do is just one of the steps on the road to "Einstein Time," but it's a big one.

How do you use time? What's your relationship with it? Is there a part of you that knows that something's got to change with you and time, but you're not changing it?

What can you do to Know your Time?

A tool to try: GATES TO THE SACRED YES — Four simple questions to take you from Sacred No (your resting place) to Sacred Yes.

How, Why, Where & When to Use It: *Some of us have our default answer as "yes."* No matter what we're asked, we say yes. If you've been a default no, switching to this strategy can flip the switch to a life well lived, as Shonda Rhimes writes in her book *My Year of Yes: How to Dance it Out, Stand in the Sun and Be Your Own Person*. But when we say yes mindlessly and reflexively, or worse from guilt and codependence, it can lead to burnout and illness. Whenever you're asked to do something, your first response can be, "Let me reflect on it and get back to you." Then sit quietly and ask yourself these questions. You can write the answers if that helps.

> Gate 1: Does it absolutely need to be done by someone?
> Gate 2: Does it absolutely need to be done now (as opposed to the future)?
> Gate 3: Does it absolutely need to be done by me?
> Gate 4: Can I do it with clarity, focus, ease, grace, and most of all, joy?

These are yes or no questions. When looking at yes or no, remember to use your primary tools. Once all four gates are passed, you are at Sacred Yes.

Affirmation

I no longer blame time for my choices.
I'm where time comes from.

Reflection Questions

- What have you discovered about yourself and your relationship with time?
- What's one area where you could stop blaming time for what you're not doing?
- If you tried Gates to the Sacred Yes, what did it show you?
- If you're a scheduler, what would you be willing to leave to chance?
- If you've avoided scheduling, what would it take to prioritize something important but not urgent?

CHAPTER 16

Know Your Integrity

Trust thyself: every heart vibrates
to that iron string.

— RALPH WALDO EMERSON[29]

Why You Must Know Your Integrity

We each have deep inner knowing. How do we access that knowing and act from it? Nowhere is this more important than in our standards of integrity. Each of us has deep standards of integrity; many of us aren't consciously in touch with what those standards are, but there's a level upon which they are operating and communicating with us all the time. Ralph Waldo Emerson's influential essay *Self-Reliance* struck me hard. I took him to mean that when we read something or hear something that strikes us as true or important, the only way that we can know that it's true or important is that it's true or important to *us*. There's really no other way.

More than ever, there are all kinds of people writing, speaking, and creating content for us. As we consume that content, some part

29 Ralph Waldo Emerson, *Self-Reliance: An Excerpt from Collected Essays, First Series*

of us is sorting it into what we like and dislike, and what is true and what is not. Emerson teaches us that the only way we know what we like and don't like or what is true and not true is by our own standards. At some level, even the standards that culture, our parents, our peers, and our religion handed to us are no match for that inner knowing. Well, maybe they are a match in the sense that people often reject their own inner knowing. We often follow what we were taught. The point of this whole book and each of its sections, but particularly this one, is to make clear that you have a choice; you can know what you know now. Whether you act upon what you know is up to you.

Stream of Consciousness Inventory: Integrity

Reputation is what men think of us;
character is what angels KNOW of us.

— THOMAS PAINE

Our inventory format for the other sections doesn't seem to work in terms of standards of integrity because each person's standards are unique to them. This section's inventory will also serve as its tool.

What I've learned about Standards of Integrity

If you spot it, you got it, that's me in the mirror.

— EVERYONE IN 12-STEP RECOVERY

"If you spot it, you got it" is often coupled with the observation that whenever I point a finger at someone else, there are three fingers pointing back at me. These adages are meant to teach us to be careful about judging, criticizing, or blaming other people. Almost invariably, the negative motives, statements, and concepts I apply to others apply to me too. In the Standards of Integrity Inventory, we will learn that "if you spot it, you got it" is equally true of positive stuff.

It turned out my standards of integrity were "influential, disciplined, ethical, visionary, and spiritual." When I learned what my standards were, I realized I wasn't actually living up to them, or at least not consistently. I would have sworn that honesty was a standard of mine; for instance, when I was about ten, on a dare, I stole a candy bar from a little store. This act tore me up. Think Raskolnikov in Dostoevsky's *Crime and Punishment.* I was up all night in terror that I would be caught and sent to prison. Honestly, you would have thought I had committed murder. The next day, I went back to the store and put a dime on the counter without saying anything and left. (Was it being out of alignment with my standard of honesty that kept me up all night? No, it was fear of being caught, but you get my point.)

I don't recall ever stealing from a merchant again, but I continued to be dishonest in various ways. As a compulsive eater, I stole food from my parents, my siblings, my roommates, my employers, and my children. As a public interest lobbyist in Washington, I would tell one member of Congress that another member of Congress had signed onto our legislation, and then when that got the first member to sign on, I would use that to get the member that I had lied to on board. It was as if Machiavelli himself had crafted my "standards of integrity" through his philosophy of "the ends justify the means." At a minimum, I lied to myself.

I judged and resented the people I worked with. I privately wrote screeds against them. I found their successes threatening. I constantly came up with new initiatives, whether they were press releases, press conferences, or goals. All of this took time and required me to constantly shift priorities. I worked insane hours and then added somewhat inappropriate social activities in the evenings. I gave no thought to the toll this might have taken on my partner or how little he saw me, how little attention he received during these times. In bars and after hours, I behaved in ways that I would now rather forget.

Which raises the question: if "influential, disciplined, ethical, visionary, and spiritual" were my standards of integrity, then why wasn't I adhering to them? Living out of alignment with my own standards took a deep toll. Without really knowing it or understanding it, the harms that I had inflicted on myself and others ate at me, so I used food, work, attention-seeking, and manipulation of other people to make myself feel better.

Even once I knew what my standards really were, I didn't suddenly behave in alignment with them. Maybe some people can do that, but I didn't. Transitioning into alignment with my standards took a lot for me. It took a deep inquiry into how I had been in the past, admitting that to a trusted person (I didn't just go straight to publishing it in a book), and then cleaning up the actions of my past. Moving forward, it took (and it still takes) daily honesty with myself and accountability with trusted people who are also trying to live in integrity. It takes the humility of knowing that it cannot be done overnight and that whatever flaws I spot in others are also in me (just as their positive qualities are in them and also me).

What can you do to know your Standards of Integrity?

A tool to try: Standards of Integrity Inventory[30]

How, Why, Where & When to Use it: Make three columns. In the first column, list five people you admire, living or dead, known only to you or famous. In the next column, list all the qualities that you admire about that particular person. In the third column, pull out all the qualities that you listed on each person and put a checkmark next to each quality that you admire for that person.

If I'm helping someone embark on any inventory where they might be looking predominantly at who they've harmed, what they did wrong, I recommend this inventory to light their way and show who they really are inside, no matter what they've done. Indeed, the reason that our past mistakes and misadventures haunt us is that they do *not* reflect who we really are. The sooner we can realize that, the better.

On the next page is an example of my Standards of Integrity Inventory.

30 Maria Nemeth, author of *The Energy of Money* — https://acecoachtraining.com/

Standards of Integrity Inventory

People I admire	Qualities that I ascribe to that person	Cumulative Qualities that I admire
Oprah	visionary, ethical, disciplined, spiritual, influential, loving	Visionary ✓✓✓✓✓✓
My father	visionary, ethical, funny, influential	Funny ✓✓✓✓
Emily Nussbaum	funny, disciplined, influential	Ethical ✓✓✓✓✓✓✓
Ralph Nader	visionary, ethical, disciplined, influential	Disciplined ✓✓✓✓✓✓
Anne Lamott	visionary, ethical, disciplined, funny, spiritual, influential, loving	Spiritual ✓✓✓✓✓
My grandmother	visionary, ethical, disciplined, funny, influential, spiritual	Influential ✓✓✓✓✓✓✓
David Alexander	visionary, ethical, disciplined, influential, spiritual, loving	Loving ✓✓✓✓
Julie Moore	Ethical, spiritual, loving	

A real inventory of my Standards of Integrity

Now, circle the top 5 qualities that reappear repeatedly in yours. Notice that in my standards inventory above, the qualities with the most checkmarks are "influential, disciplined, ethical, visionary, and spiritual." So whatever yours are, you would write them out on a piece of paper (or a note on your phone or wherever you'll see it) like this:

These are my standards of integrity:

Influential
Disciplined
Ethical
Visionary
Spiritual

I know they are mine because I recognize them in others.

Now, as you walk through the world, keep those standards of integrity close at hand. Read them every day. Repeat all the words on the card. Recite your standards of integrity, and affirm that you know they are yours because you recognize them in others.

Affirmation

I NOW KNOW WHO I AM AND WHY I AM HERE. I LET MY STANDARDS OF INTEGRITY LIGHT THE WAY FOR ME IN LIFE, AS A PATH FOR ME AND OTHERS TO FOLLOW.

Reflection Questions

- Now that you know your Standards of Integrity, without beating yourself up, take a look at each standard. What do you see?
- To what degree are you aligned with that standard?
- Where are you out of alignment with it?
- What, if anything, are you willing to straighten out? (*Hint: Sometimes it's enough to just be in the question.*)

CHAPTER 17

Know Your Boundaries

Boundaries are anything that help to differentiate you from someone else, or show where you begin and end.[31]

— DR. HENRY CLOUD & DR. JOHN TOWNSEND

Why you need to know Boundaries

If you roll your eyes when people bring up the topic of "boundaries," chances are you naturally know where you end and other people begin. Some of us are naturals at keeping ourselves healthy, whole, and saf,e and letting others take care of their own needs. Others, probably due to messages from our broader or micro culture or family of origin, or because that's what we perceived was necessary to keep ourselves alive, learned to focus on the happiness and safety of others as a way of guaranteeing our own safety, if not happiness. We thought that for us to be safe, someone else had to be pacified; for us to be okay, someone else's needs had to be met.

As we became adults and lived our own lives, we also learned to

---

31 *Boundaries: When to Say Yes, How to Say No to take control of your life* by Dr. Henry Cloud and Dr. John Townsend

blame others for our poor life skills. Because someone else's needs come first (a parent, a child, a partner, a boss), we are unable to eat healthily, exercise well, get enough sleep, or do what we are here to do.

The more we recognize ourselves and how we've been with boundaries, the more we can stand in our own power and authority, allowing others to be in theirs. That shift can be transformative to many relationships.

Stream of Consciousness Inventory: Boundaries

Boundaries help us keep the good in and the bad out.[32]

To find out how powerful your Boundaries & Communication stream flows, rate each statement below on a scale of 1 to 5 according to how true/light that statement is for you. 5 indicates the statement is totally true/light, and one indicates that it is false/heavy. Add up your first five ratings to get your FLOW # and the second set of five ratings to get your GROW #. Subtract your GROW # from your FLOW # to get your current Boundaries & Communication Stream Power.

Assign a number to each statement below on how true/light the statement feels for you, 5 being the most true.

___ I am responsible for my own happiness, not other people's happiness.

___ I know the difference between hurt and harm. Taking care of myself might hurt someone, but it will never harm them.

32 *Boundaries*, Cloud and Townsend

___ I can say no without an explanation of why I'm saying no.

___ I know my limits with other people and I'm able to honor them.

___ I know that boundaries are fences, not walls. Because I can hold a boundary, I don't always have to cut problematic people out of my life. I do what I can do with them and not what I can't.

For the five statements above, calculate your **FLOW #** _____

We judge the boundary decisions of others, thinking that we know best how they "ought" to give, and usually that means "they ought to give to me the way I want them to!"[33]

___ The people who drive me crazy are the problem. I am at their mercy.

___ If the people in my life don't stop doing the things they do to hurt me, I will cut them off.

___ Setting a boundary is telling another person what they need to start or stop doing so that I can be okay.

___ My happiness depends on the happiness of my family or friends.

___ It's not up to me to keep myself safe, it's up to others to stop hurting me.

For the five statements above, calculate your **GROW #** _____

33 *Boundaries*, Cloud and Townsend

Subtract your GROW # from your FLOW # to find out your KNOW # for your Boundaries & Communication.

FLOW - GROW = _______ KNOW

Congratulations to you for taking the time to know this aspect of yourself. You now know so much more about what you know and what you don't know about Boundaries & Communication.

If your KNOW # is 17-25, your stream of consciousness on Boundaries & Communication has a powerful flow.

If your KNOW # is 8-16, your stream of consciousness on this topic is steady but could be stronger if that's something you'd like.

If your KNOW # is from less than less than 0 to 7, your stream of consciousness on this topic is at a trickle.

What I've learned about Boundaries

> "Well, have you ever gone to the dentist?" I asked.
>
> "Sure."
>
> "Did the dentist hurt you when he drilled your tooth to remove the cavity?"
>
> "Yes."
>
> "Did he harm you?"
>
> "No, he made me feel better."[34]

Boundaries can hurt, but they can't harm

While every inventory we take in this book is a chance to move from unconsciousness to consciousness, the inventories about what

34 *Boundaries*, Cloud and Townsend

we know in relationships and people may be the hardest to navigate. Let me assure you that seeing how we've been can be liberating.

I probably never heard my mother utter the word "boundary," but she certainly didn't like them. She was a pioneer teacher of classrooms without walls. She believed that bedtimes, food restrictions, and deciding what children should or shouldn't learn in school were harmful. I wasn't allowed to keep the door to my room or the bathroom closed growing up. Quite literally. After having come home in 2nd grade with stomach aches due to a cruel teacher, my parents transferred me for 3rd grade to "the Exploring Family School"—a private venture in the 1960s, which they were part of, that took 50 kids ages 5 to 18 and stuck us in and around a barn with three teachers. While most of the kids seemed content to run around building forts and showing each other their private parts, I compelled one of the teachers to sit inside the barn with me day after day to teach me algebra (since those were the only school books they had). The following year, I demanded to be back in the normal 4th grade.

From then on out, I moved towards self-sufficiency to protect myself against further incursions. If mom was going to subject me to a relentless stream of questions about what I was wearing, eating, or doing, I was going to be elsewhere. I enrolled in a series of dance and performance arts classes and took the bus as my mode of transportation. Once old enough, I took jobs for every spare moment that I wasn't rehearsing; then I went away to college, followed by law school, and mostly stayed away except for winter holidays.

Since mom took every boundary I set or held personally, those "boundaries" turned into walls. At the same time, I judged and took personally the boundaries of others, especially the man who would become my spouse, who embodied not only *boundaries* but *self-discipline.* "What kind of sick game is he playing?" I would wonder when he got up early to exercise and eat a healthy meal before facing the day. What did he mean we'd divide up shopping and meal preparation and decide our meals in advance? Why did he think it was okay to restrict dining to the dining room or kitchen when I was accustomed to taking my food to my room or the TV to escape or tune out?

Over time, I learned that a) boundaries can be held, b) my "boundaries" were not fences but walls designed to keep people out, and c) that there were more than two impossible choices: keep them happy or keep them away. These lessons allow me an increasing connection with other people, where I can "say what I mean, and not say it mean,"[35] plus let others live their lives and have feelings without taking those personally.

What can you do to know your Boundaries?

A tool to try: YOU MAY BE RIGHT — "You May Be Right" is both something you can literally say to others when you don't know what to say and a tool for generating new ideas on what to say or how to act with people who you keep allowing to harm you.

How, Why, Where & When to Use it: When you repeatedly interact with a certain person (often a family member, but sometimes a coworker or someone else) and you find yourself allowing them to harm you in various ways, this is a tool you can use to access your inner wisdom and come up with new ideas.

35 a saying taught in Al-Anon Family Groups https://al-anon.org/

What They Do or Say	What I Usually Do or Say	What I Can Do or Say Instead
State political opinions you strongly disagree with	Argue with them	Say "You may be right" or "can you believe it?" (and then change the subject, see below)
You need to come help me with this	I'll be right there	Sorry, that won't work for me
So and so is a problem because blah blah blah	Listen for a while and then argue with them about it	Change the subject abruptly the minute they start down this road to something you can stand to hear about: Their pet, their grandchild, anything
Attack you emotionally	Argue with them or let them, either way, feel bad	If you live with them and you're at home, say "Oops gotta go!" and run to the bathroom. If they're on the phone, say "Oh wow, something just came up. Gotta go. Bye!" and hang up.

Using something like the sample chart, write down what people say or do that troubles you. Put what you generally say or do in the second column, and then what you potentially could say or do in the 3rd column. By giving you a sample, I'm sneaking in some of the ideas that I've come up with or have been suggested to me over the years, and although the point of this book is to know what *you* know.

In learning to hold boundaries when we haven't been able to before, it can be very useful to ask for help from someone, perhaps a member of Al-Anon Family Groups[36] for friends and family members of Alcoholics (or addicts), or Codependents Anonymous, or a therapist. You can also use the Light vs. Heavy tool to determine whether it feels right for you to seek help from those resources.

Obviously, you can add more rows to this chart and edit the examples to suit your situation.

Affirmation

I KNOW WHERE I END AND OTHERS BEGIN.

I NO LONGER RELY ON OTHERS TO DETERMINE THAT FOR ME.

Reflection Questions

- Do you say yes and then resent saying yes for fear of losing someone's love?
- Do you feel a burden to pay for all you have been given?
- Does the boundary you are holding hurt them (cause them feelings), or does it just harm them?
- How did the "You May Be Right" tool work for you?

36 Al-Anon Family Groups https://al-anon.org/

CHAPTER 18

Know Your Reality

When God is left out, reality just boils down to personal feelings, opinions, illusions, structures, superstition, and chaos—nothing more. Reality is so much more. It is a living miracle if you would only behold it!

-ATTRIBUTED TO JESUS BY GLENDA GREEN[37]

Why you need to know your Reality

One very tricky part of knowing what you know is whether you can believe your own senses and whether that is part of the knowing. The truth is that you can and you can't believe your own senses. I can believe that my eyes are perceiving a tree outside my window, blue jeans on my body, people sleeping on the streets of my city, newspapers reporting that U.S. citizens are being picked up on the streets without due process and detained indefinitely.

All of that is, for sure, my perception. But does that make it "real"? The Sanskrit word *Maya* means "magic" or "illusion" — the

37 *Love Without End: Jesus Speaks* by Glenda Green

unreality of what appears real. Essentially, Maya is the living dream of the world.

Just as our nighttime dreams appear totally real to us with people and adventures all projected from our consciousness, so many thinkers, eastern and western alike, believe that the "real world" is actually a projection of our individual and/or collective consciousness or, perhaps more accurately, unconscious. Quantum Science backs up this understanding. Everything in our conscious *and* subconscious minds is creating our world and our reality.

For that reason, *knowing* is a way to get underneath our limited perceptions fueled by implanted ideas to reality. Let's take a look at what you know is real or isn't.

Stream of Consciousness Inventory: Reality

The world is full of magic things, patiently waiting for our senses to grow sharper.

- WILLIAM BUTLER YEATS

To find out how powerful your reality stream flows, rate each statement below on a scale of 1 to 5 according to how true/light that statement is for you. 5 indicates the statement is totally true/light, and one indicates that it is false/heavy. Add up your first five ratings to get your FLOW # and the second set of five ratings to get your GROW #. Subtract your GROW # from your FLOW # to get your current Reality Stream Power.

Assign a number to each statement below on how true/light the statement feels for you, 5 being the most true.

___ I understand that all of "reality" is a projection of my consciousness.

___ Because reality is a projection of my consciousness, that means that both poverty, war, and racism as well as abundance, joy, and love emanate from me. What I see comes through my knowing.

___ My work is to understand that both are true so that I don't blame or shame the apparent reality, whatever it is.

___ I take responsibility for the reality I perceive.

___ And I work to create in consciousness the new reality that I want to see.

For the five statements above, calculate your **FLOW #** _____

We need to stop being surprised or shocked by reality and recognize that evil flourishes best when it is denied. Evil relies on being considered rational, necessary, and expedient by otherwise good people.

-RICHARD ROHR[38]

___ I don't believe anything unless I see it with my own eyes.

___ Reality is happening to me, my mind is not making it up.

___ If I feel it, I know it's true. It's that simple.

___ The only reality is the reality I perceive with my conscious mind. The unconscious is all BS.

38 *The Tears of Things: Prophetic Wisdom for an Age of Outrage* by Richard Rohr

___ The bad things I see or experience were created by someone else, never by me.

For the 5 statements above, calculate your **GROW #** _____

Subtract your GROW # from your FLOW # to find out your KNOW # for your Reality.

FLOW - GROW = _______ KNOW

If your KNOW # is 17-25, congratulations, you've learned that at the level of the Reality you're actually enjoying all of it, even the parts you're not "supposed" to. You just might be a *Super Streamer* of Reality.

If your KNOW # is 8-16, you know that Reality is affected by perception but you don't know how to altar your perception or take responsibility for Reality.

If your KNOW # is from less than 0 to 7, it could be an indication that see yourself as a victim of Reality.

What I've learned about Reality

One of the things that made Jesus' words so alive was his conviction in reality. To him, God is not only real, but also the source of reality and the highest reality

— GLENDA GREEN

When I was a kid, my mother constantly questioned my own version of reality. Whatever I said my feelings were, I was told they were wrong and that wasn't it. So it was confusing weaving recovery into my therapy where I had to now admit that everything I had characterized about the way people had treated me might be wrong.

Sometimes I'll believe that the furniture in my room is real, and the news (whatever the source) is real, but I won't believe that my subconscious mind is real.

As this book is about *knowing what you know,* we must know the difference between "fake reality" and "real reality." Otherwise, we could be operating from what we *think* we know, or what we think we *should* know.

Knowing what we know is one of the ways to tell the difference between the fake and real realities or to transition from the fake/minerva to the real/nirvana — it's a shuttle, a transportation point.

This is what quantum physicists refer to as a "tangled hierarchy"—like the Escher print with the two hands drawing each other–I need to *know what I know* to tell the difference between fake and real realities, and I need to know the difference between fake and real realities to *know what I know.*

Quantum physics tells us that the reality we see and sense and believe to be real is simply projected by human agreement and consciousness. It can all change in an instant. We think that only actions in the real world can change reality.

For example, my irritating neighbor will only cease to be irritating if:

a) they move
b) they go to a therapist or enter recovery and do deep work or
c) they die.

I don't want to consider the possibility that they will cease to be irritating when I stop seeing them as irritating. But the old saw, "my how you've changed, since I've changed," operates here.

Which brings us back to what has often been observed: the unconscious mind is basically the rest of the iceberg, the part we can't see above the surface. Since everything we perceive is a projection of our consciousness, it stands to reason that the giant, dark unconscious mind some call "THE Reality" is a massive, hidden operating system and driver of what we think we know. However, it's very tricky because, unlike the *conscious* mind, where we may not know what we know, but we do have some handle on knowing what we *think* or *think we know*, the Reality or unconscious mind is hidden from us. If that's so, I could use the next Tool or do equivalent work and not experience a fundamental shift in my perception of my neighbor because at the level of the unconscious, *I may not want to have a shift.* My Reality self may be having a great time being irritated by my neighbor. I may be secretly unconsciously thrilled every time they send an annoying email or do something outrageous.

So sometimes *knowing what we know* is a process of deduction—if I am repeatedly resenting or envying or acting out in an addictive pattern or I'm perpetually financially strapped or anything, and judging or hating or shaming myself over it, I can surmise that there is something that I am really enjoying about repeating that process and hating myself.[39]

39 *Existential Kink* by Carolyn Elliott, PhD

What can you do to know your Reality?

A tool to try: RECLAIMING "REALITY" — Reclaim (your real) Reality by telling your apparent reality/story and reclaiming your power from it.

How, Why, Where & When to Use it: Use this powerful tool whenever you find yourself feeling victimized or powerless in what you perceive to be "the reality." To perceive ourselves as victims, we must have given our power away to the story and believed it more than we believed ourselves. This straightforward process invites us to briefly tell the story of how it feels to us now and then to express or acknowledge the truth of the situation by saying aloud statements of truth, acknowledging what we are coming to know of ourselves. The following statements are adapted from *Busting Loose from the Money Game.*[40]

I AM THE PRESENCE and POWER of GOD'S ABUNDANCE who created the apparent reality. (Now tell what's going on from your victim perspective.):

- But it's Not REAL, it's **MY STORY.**
- It's Completely Made Up, it's **MY STORY.**
- It's been a CREATION from my CURRENT state of **CONSCIOUSNESS.**
- However, I **NOW RECLAIM MY POWER** from this "made up" STORY.

40 Adapted by Allie Singer from "The Process" in *Busting Loose from the Money Game* by Robert Scheinfeld

- As **I RECLAIM MY POWER**, I feel **ALL MY POWER** coming back to me.
- I feel **ALL MY POWER SURGING THROUGH ME.**
- As I feel the surge, I feel myself **EXPANDING** into who I **TRULY AM,** and I express more and more of who **I TRULY AM** in my HUMAN EXPERIENCE.

After reclaiming your power from the apparent reality, affirm your truth and give thanks by saying:

Affirmation

(which in this case is part of the above tool, hence long)

I AM THE PRESENCE AND POWER OF GOD'S ABUNDANCE. AS SUCH, I FULLY APPRECIATE HOW AMAZING I AM. IT WAS JUST MY STORY. IT'S TRULY AMAZING HOW CREATIVE I AM AND HOW BEAUTIFULLY EVERYTHING WORKS IN MY LIFE TO SERVE ME AND IS CREATED BY ME, FOR ME. I AM GRATEFUL MY CONSCIOUSNESS HAS NOW EXPANDED INTO WHO I TRULY AM. THANK YOU GOD!

Reflection Questions

- What, if anything has shifted in your perception of reality now (either from this reading or other stuff)?
- What makes sense to you about the effect your consciousness can have upon your perception of "reality"?
- What do you know or believe about what's real and what's not?

CHAPTER 19

Know Your Caregiving

With Real Love, there is no disappointment,
impatience, irritation, or anger.
Wow, now that is different—so different that
most people have never truly felt it.

— GREG BAER, MD

Why you need to know your Caregiving

This section is for anyone who is or has cared for children of any age, grand, step or foster, or whether those "children" used to be your parents and now are yours to care for. Whoever you're caring for, even if only younger versions of yourself, you may benefit from knowing more about your true role, rather than your idea of the role.

Most of us grew up with highly conditional love; yet, as discussed, true love is, by definition, unconditional. Earlier in this book, we learned more about a form of unconditional love known as "boundaries." Boundaries are not conditional, but they are relational.

In this section, we'll explore how we enable the people we care for to be heroes on their journey, experiencing the natural consequences of their actions. Or, put another way, we'll see whether we're allowing them to know what they *know*. Perhaps we'll get a better understanding of where we are on a continuum of transactional to unconditional love or attachment to our roles.

Stream of Consciousness Inventory: Caregiving

Love is by definition unconditional, so we don't say "unconditional love."

— SISTER SHIVANI

To find out how powerful your Caregiving stream flows, rate each statement below on a scale of 1 to 5 according to how true/light that statement is for you. 5 indicates the statement is totally true/light, and one indicates that it is false/heavy. Add up your first five ratings to get your FLOW # and the second set of five ratings to get your GROW #. Subtract your GROW # from your FLOW # to get your current Caregiving Stream Power.

Assign a number to each statement below on how true/light the statement feels for you, 5 being the most true.

___ I am aware of my family member's or friend's problematic ways, but I don't have to judge them.

___ The people I'm caring for are heroes on their own journeys with their own answers no matter what their age or condition.

___ I am responsible for my own happiness, not theirs.

___ I can and do forgive the people that hurt me.

___ My closest family or friends drive me crazy regularly, so there's something wrong with me.

For the five statements above, calculate your **FLOW #** _____

Ego is attachment to a wrong image of myself, my home, my body, my role, my position, my caste.

— SISTER SHIVANI

___ I have to keep my loved ones safe at all costs, if anything at all hurts them, it's on me.

___ I get angry when people around me don't follow the rules we've agreed to.

___ I cook and I clean and pay the rent, the least they could do is be nice to me.

___ I just wish I could be more patient and loving.

___ I am the caregiver so I have to be the one to do everything and know everything.

For the five statements above, calculate your **GROW #** _____

Subtract your GROW # from your FLOW # to find out your KNOW # for your Caregiving

FLOW - GROW = _______ KNOW

Congratulations to you for taking the time to know this aspect of yourself. You now know so much more about what you know and what you don't know about Caregiving.

If your KNOW # is 17-25, your stream of consciousness on Caregiving has a powerful flow.

If your KNOW # is 8-16, your stream of consciousness on this topic is steady but could be stronger if that's something you'd like.

If your KNOW # is from less than 0 to 7, your stream of consciousness on this topic is at a trickle.

What I've learned about Caregiving

We are to love one another, not be one another. I can't feel your feelings for you. I can't think for you. I can't behave for you. I can't work through the disappointment that limits bring for you. In short, I can't grow for you; only you can.[41]

In his series on Real Love,[42] Dr. Greg Baer tells his story of how he, a married top surgeon and father of six children, found himself in his backyard with a shotgun in his mouth and addicted to opioids. He quit medicine and became interested in how we can actually show up in "real" (or unconditional) love in our various relationships. Like some of us, Greg had to hit bottom to get in touch with what he knew, which was that what he craved (and perhaps what all people crave) is unconditional love.

These books, and my own life experience, taught me that almost nobody has experienced real (or unconditional) love. Love for most of us has been transactional. From, "I'll love you if you clean your room, get straight A's, and eat your vegetables," to "I'll love you if you come home by curfew time," to "I'll love you if you stop driving and never walk without a walker."

As a mother of two children, one of whom was sick for years, and as the daughter of a woman who lived with Alzheimer's disease

41 *Boundaries* by Cloud and Townsend

42 *Real Love in Marriage, Real Love in Dating, Real Love in Parenting, Real Love in the Workplace* by Greg Baer, MD

for years, I had ample opportunity to test my abilities as a caregiver (hence my ability to love). Dr. Baer's practical tips for allowing children to experience the consequences of their actions changed me as a mother.[43] For example, previously, I would scold and make my children feel bad if they failed to hang their suits and towels up to dry after swim practice. Then I would resent them, as I was the one who hung the suits up or put them in the dryer. As a result, their behavior never changed, and none of us enjoyed the run-up to swimming.

When I started getting out of the way and letting them see what it felt like to wear and use their cold, damp suit and towels for practice (with no scolding or commenting on it, just observation), they quickly started hanging up their own suits and towels.

When my mother first showed evidence of dementia, I immediately wanted to leap in and control every aspect of her life. With children, it *is* my job as a parent to decide what is an acceptable risk for them to take and what is not. Some elements of control may be necessary to keep them from running into traffic when they're little or coming to other preventable harm. Yet, as children age, some parents tend to continue to keep very tight reins on behavior, believing that the single most important aspect of parenting is to keep a child alive.

On the other end of life, a similar trajectory can begin. As a parent's memory, judgment, and balance may start to falter, the adult child may appoint themselves caregiver before the parent is ready or willing to accept that change in role. I had to learn over and over

43 Had any of us paid more attention to the children's book series with Mrs. Piggle-Wiggle, we likely wouldn't have needed *Real Love*. Mrs. Piggle-Wiggle would coach parents on how to address their children's bad habits, almost always through logical (but hilarious) consequences. One kid who wouldn't clean up his room was allowed to let the room get so messy he couldn't leave it until he finally had to clean it up just to come out and get food.

that my mother had been an adult and *my* parent for over 50 years, and that even if some of her abilities were changing, as long as she was cognizant of the risks of falling when going up and down stairs unassisted, it was not my decision whether she did it. If she didn't want help with her life activities, so long as she was mostly in her right mind, that was not my business either.

Allowing children and parents (appropriate to their abilities) to make their own mistakes and face their own consequences is not only unconditionally loving, but it is also a demonstration that we know that *they* know and we respect it.

Sister Shivani's quotes above reflect the Hindu perspective that we are all souls who come into a body with certain goals and missions. Those souls in bodies are called people and sometimes cluster together in relationships in families. So it may appear that there are these fixed roles called Mother, Father, Child, or Sibling, and that each role has a particular job or responsibility for these other souls in bodies. The truth may be that while we appear to be 5, 28, 45, or 89 years old, that is just our bodies. We may also be 100s of years old as souls and have particular missions here on earth.

Indeed, before she had symptoms of dementia, I used to try so hard to make my mother happy, and it never seemed to work. I once organized a whole reunion of my mother's side of the family "for her" on the East Coast (my mother had spent her whole adult life on the West Coast of the United States, while the rest of her siblings and nieces and nephews were in the southeastern U.S.). It was a wonderful reunion, and we all enjoyed it, but our mother complained bitterly about multiple aspects of it. I don't even remember what she didn't like, but it was clear that the reunion "hadn't worked" because she wasn't happy.

This was just one event in a series of experiences my mother and I "enjoyed" in this lifetime until a mentor suggested that maybe my mother didn't want to be happy. Wow. What a lightbulb turned on for me at that time. I realized that my mother's mission on earth might have been to be unhappy. And that I didn't have either the responsibility or even the *right* to get in the way of her life's purpose. From that point on, to respect and acknowledge what she knew, I endeavored to catch and release myself from that compulsion going forward.

Had I understood or employed the tool of Light vs. Heavy earlier on, I would have felt clearly that it was never "light" for me to try to make her happy. But what was light now was the ability to live life the way she wanted, within certain bounds. If she wanted to go to Trader Joe's every day and buy the exact same products she already had in the fridge, oh well. If she wanted to water her plants 25 times a day and kill those plants, so be it. If she tried to feed her dog bacon and cheese at every meal, that was a slightly different matter, because it hurt the dog.

What can you do to know your Caregiving?

A tool to try: LET THEM KNOW WHAT THEY KNOW — Focus on knowing what you know and let them focus on knowing what they know by stopping the five Ms: managing, manipulating, martyring, mothering, or monitoring.[44]

How, Why, Where & When to Use it: Letting go of the five Ms (by letting them know what they know) is helpful in any relationship, but particularly when it comes to parenting children or parents. The main thing to "do" is not to do unless truly necessary. As long as it

44 *Pathways to Recovery* Al-Anon Family Groups

will not harm someone else, or as the harm to themselves is not truly our responsibility, let our children, our parents and those we are caring for know what they know and do what they do no matter how stupid or weird or wasteful it seems. If they don't ask us for help, let them be and do what they're being and doing.

Note: If you consistently find that you cannot refrain from managing, manipulating, martyring, mothering, or monitoring the behavior of people who are not children under 10 and that bothers you, consider visiting Al-Anon Family Groups https://al-anon.org/ to learn how to let them.

Affirmation

I KNOW WHAT I KNOW, AND I LET OTHERS KNOW WHAT THEY KNOW. THEY ARE HEROES ON THEIR OWN JOURNEY, GUIDED BY THEIR OWN INNER WISDOM.

Reflection Questions

- Am I truly concerned about the people I'm caring for, or am I more worried about myself?
- What could it be like if I truly saw the people around me as heroes on their own journeys?
- What if I saw myself, my children, and the people I'm caring for as other souls instead of as a certain role?
- What stops me? What am I afraid of?

CHAPTER 20

Know Your Beliefs

Go! Let it be done just as you believed it would.

— MATTHEW[45]

Why You Must Know Your Beliefs

The great spiritual scientist Jesus the Christ said, "It is done unto you as you believe"; yet how many of us systematically pay attention to what we believe, so that we know how it will be done?

The idea that it is done as you believe isn't just spiritual science, it's hard science; the pharmaceutical industry has such a hard time proving that its medications work better than a sugar pill (which test subjects have been told will cure them—also known as "the placebo effect") that it routinely petitions the Food and Drug Administration to remove that requirement for approval.

In plain speech, that means that decades of scientific research and profit incentive can't beat the power of your mind to heal your body (or do anything else it thinks it can do). The ability of your mind to

45 Matthew 8:13 NIV

achieve anything depends on your beliefs. The more you believe you can do something, the more you can. It's as simple as that.

Changing beliefs can be done, but it's challenging. Sometimes, the easiest path to manifesting what you want is by focusing on the best thing that you already believe in. To do that, you have to know what you believe. Shall we look into what we believe together?

Stream of Consciousness Inventory: Beliefs

Mindfulness is a way of befriending ourselves and our experience.

— JON KABAT-ZINN

This inventory will be a little different. Most of the other inventories have been just to know more about our default thoughts, opinions, and conclusions. In this inventory, we're looking more at the strength of our beliefs. To find out how powerful your Belief stream flows, rate each statement below on a scale of 1 to 5 according to how true/light that statement is for you. 5 indicates the statement is totally true/light, and one indicates that it is false/heavy. Add up your first five ratings to get your FLOW # and the second set of five ratings to get your GROW #. Subtract your GROW # from your FLOW # to get your current Belief Stream Power.

Assign a number to each statement below on how true/light the statement feels for you, 5 being the most true.

___ I can heal my body, bank account, relationships, or the world just with the power of my mind.

___ I can integrate a new suggestion about how to heal my body, bank account, relationships or the world and it will work.

___ I can't heal any of those things, but there are people who can, and I can find them or they will find me.

___ Whether I'm sick or well, rich or poor, happy or sad is all in God's hands (but I trust God and that's fine).

___ Whether I'm sick or well, rich or poor, happy or sad it's all completely random chance.

For the five statements above, calculate your **FLOW #** _____

"Whether you think you can, or think you can't — you're right," is a powerful quote attributed to Henry Ford. For the purpose of this exercise, I've tweaked it some for you to consider.

If I believe I can't do it, I'm right.

___ I can't heal my body, bank account, relationships, or the world just with the power of my mind.

___ I can't read or learn a suggestion about how to heal my body, bank account, relationships or the world, and implement it such that it works.

___ I can't heal any of those things, some people do that, but I can't find them.

___ Whether I'm sick or well, rich or poor, happy or sad is all in God's hands.

___ Whether I'm sick or well, rich or poor, happy or sad it's all completely random chance.

For the five statements above, calculate your **GROW #** _____

Subtract your GROW # from your FLOW # to find out your KNOW # for your Beliefs.

FLOW - GROW = _______ KNOW

Congratulations to you for taking the time to know this aspect of yourself. You now know so much more about what you know and what you don't know about Beliefs.

If your KNOW # is 17-25, your stream of consciousness on Beliefs has a powerful flow.

If your KNOW # is 8-16, your stream of consciousness on this topic is steady but could be stronger if that's something you'd like.

If your KNOW # is from less than 0 to 7, your stream of consciousness on this topic is at a trickle.

What I've Learned about Beliefs

Since beliefs shape how life unfolds, it can be interesting and rewarding to learn a way to change or work with existing beliefs. The more we know what we know, the more we can replace beliefs that don't serve us with beliefs that do. But this is a process, and it doesn't necessarily happen overnight. Science of Mind, which the Centers for Spiritual Living (where I am an ordained minister) teaches, favors affirmation and "spiritual mind treatment" as a way to change beliefs. Some of the Access Consciousness tools we're exploring, such as the question, "What else is possible?", aim to quickly eradicate harmful beliefs or bypass our belief system altogether.

Changing beliefs can be done, but it's challenging. Despite years of training and schooling in spiritual manifestation techniques, sometimes I still don't believe that I can sit in a room and chant, "I am well. I am whole. I am well," or "This is a loving, caring country that works for everyone," and just suddenly perceive those affirmations to be true. An author and speaker named Terry McBride taught me that sometimes the easiest path to manifesting what I want is to identify and focus on the best/most useful thing that I already believe. He learned this when, as a young man, he was told that most of his bones were so deeply infected that doctors predicted he'd never walk again, would live with a colostomy bag, and have zero sexual function. Being a young man, the last point was what really got his attention. Spiritual scientists around him prayed and affirmed, "You are healthy, you are whole," over him, but that didn't work. McBride realized that the reason it didn't work was that he didn't believe it. Maybe they did, but he didn't. So he examined what he *did* believe would work and asked a lot more questions. The doctor admitted reluctantly that there was an experimental surgery to remove infection from bone marrow, but that it was hugely expensive only one surgeon knew how to perform it, and that surgeon was in high demand internationally. That didn't matter to Terry. He realized that he believed with certainty that he could convince this surgeon to do the surgery and that somehow it would be paid for. He focused on that belief and had surgery after surgery with the right surgeon. Several surgeries were needed over the course of years. In so doing, he was completely healed and walked and digested with ease for the rest of a long life.

This was the story I needed to hear at the time, after years of worry about our child. I focused on the phrase, "There is a professional who can heal my loved one, and I can easily find them." In less than a day, the name came, we met the physician, and in less than two weeks, my family member was back to full health for a couple of years.

Despite my background, I've never been crazy about affirmations (and as a result, I've rarely seen results with them). But at one point many years ago, I learned another tool from Maria Nemeth that I call "the Thinking Person's affirmation" – gathering evidence for a new conclusion. So I'm going to introduce you to that tool now.

What can you do to know your Beliefs?

A tool to try: WHAT'S THE BEST THING YOU BELIEVE? — Zero in on the beliefs that serve you rather than those that don't.

How, Why, Where & When to Use it: You have a goal. Maybe it's to publish a book. You don't know where to start. Well, maybe you can do what I did: inventory and examine my beliefs to find the ones that were most useful. Often, the beliefs build on each other. Other people are wild about self-publishing. For many reasons, that idea just repelled me. I wasn't impressed by several self-published books I read, nor by their distribution. So that was one belief.

Given that I didn't believe in self-publishing, I needed a way to find a publisher. I didn't know how to go about getting/finding a publisher. However, I believed that I could find someone who could coach me in that area. So, given that I didn't believe in self-publishing, that was a useful belief to stack on top of the other one.

So, I focused both my inner and outer work on finding a coach who could help me find a publisher. Within days, I had found one, and you are now reading the results of that work.

So how do you do this? Take a given area where you want to manifest or change something. Write a list of all the things you believe about your ability to manifest or change that something. Don't try to distinguish whether those beliefs are *helpful* or not. Just make a list. Like, if you're trying to figure out your next career, you might brainstorm a list like this.

Things I believe about finding my next career:

- I need to get another degree.
- It will be expensive.
- I have only myself to depend on.
- I can't afford more than two years of additional education.
- I can do and enjoy lots of different work.
- The right choice exists for me.
- I know someone right now who is knowledgeable about this, or knows someone who is knowledgeable about this.
- Somehow, the name of the right person to talk to will come to me at the right time.

Now take a look at that list above. This list may not accurately reflect a list *you* would write, but it is a good example of what I, or many of my clients, might believe about themselves. Notice that many of the beliefs, while they may be "well-founded," might not be all that useful to focus on. For example, people often decide in advance that a new career requires a new professional degree, or that getting a new degree is beyond their economic reach. Both of those beliefs might wither if subjected to scrutiny and accurate research, but as we've discussed above, people don't easily allow their beliefs to be changed.

Now, move your finger down the list and, using the Light vs. Heavy or Candle Flame tool, dial in on which option feels the lightest (or generates the strongest candle flame) for you to focus on. The question you're asking yourself is really, "What's the best (or most useful) belief I have on this question?"

Which belief stands out? Let's say it was, "Somehow the name of the right person will come to me." Now *that's* the belief you focus your prayers, your intentions, and your *curiosity* on.

Affirmation

WHATEVER BELIEF I FOCUS ON WILL COME TO FRUITION, SO I FOCUS ON THE BEST THING I BELIEVE.

Reflection Questions

- What do you believe is the relationship between your beliefs and how your life outpictures?
- What experience can you think of where you focused on the worst thing you believed (often called "worrying")?
- What about focusing on the best thing – what's happened when you've done that (or what do you imagine will happen)?

CHAPTER 21

Know Your Death

The fear of death follows from the fear of life.
A man who lives fully is prepared to die at any time.

— MARK TWAIN

Why you need to know your Death

Even though everyone dies and everyone is born, in Western culture, we focus a lot more on birth than death. Births are wonderful and to be embraced. Death is bad news and to be avoided–like that. The ancient cultures of the world celebrate death as part of life and don't shy away from talking about it with people of all ages. Where are you on that? If we don't know where we are in death, we don't know where we are in life. I assume you're here to live life to the fullest.

Stream of Consciousness Inventory: Death

Until we can entrust ourselves to death,
we never really entrust ourselves to life.

— SALLIE NICHOLS[46]

To find out how aware you are of your ideas about death, rate each statement below on a scale of 1 to 5 according to how light that statement is for you. 5 indicates the statement is totally light (so it could feel very light and expansive, that's our yes/truth), and 1 indicates that it is heavy and stuck (that's our no/false). Add up your first five ratings to get your FLOW # and the second set of five ratings to get your GROW #. Subtract your GROW # from your KNOW # to get your current Death Awareness Flow.

Assign a number between 1 and 5 to each statement below on how true/light the statement feels for you with 5 being the most true, 1 being the least true.

___ I know that anyone can die at any time and that thought causes me to live life to the fullest.
___ I am at peace with my own death whenever it happens.
___ I have thoroughly mourned the people I love who have already died.
___ When people I know lose someone they love, I am able to communicate my condolences directly.
___ Births are fun and happy. Deaths are bad and scary.

For the five statements above, calculate your **FLOW #** _____

46 Author of *Jung and Tarot: An Archetypal Journey*

Death is not the biggest fear we have; our biggest fear is taking the risk to be alive—the risk to be alive and express what we really are.

— MIGUEL ANGEL RUIZ

___ The knowledge that anyone can die at any time terrifies and paralyzes me.
___ I see no point in talking or thinking about death. It's morbid.
___ Every year when certain death dates roll around, I can barely function because I'm so overcome with grief.
___ I don't really grieve. The dead are dead. I just move on.
___ Every time someone I love dies, it puts in perspective all the little things that I worry and think about (but then I forget).

Subtract your GROW # from your FLOW # to find out your KNOW # for your Death on Death's Terms.

FLOW - GROW = ______ KNOW

If your KNOW # is 17-25, congratulations, you're aware of what your thoughts and beliefs are about death, what you know, and maybe even what you don't know, and you are present to how that points to living life to the fullest. You just might be a *Super Streamer* of Death on Death's Terms.

If your KNOW # is 8-16, you know some of what you know about death, but a bunch is hidden from you.

If your KNOW # is from less than 0 to 7, it could be an indication that you are avoiding knowing what you know about death.

What I've Learned about Death

Krishnamurti was asked how he went about preparing himself for death. To this he replied: "Each day I die a little."

— SALLIE NICHOLS

Speaking with some longtime friends recently, I realized, not for the first time, that I'm (at least consciously) pretty surrendered to the idea that I and everyone around me are going to die. But many people either avoid thinking about their death or other people's, or actively fear everything to do with it, or both, of course, since those choices are not mutually exclusive.

Where are you on this? Chances are, like most things in life, your experience has shaped your feelings. When I was two and a half, my baby brother Phillip died at two months old. When I was 23, our father died at age 55. Both deaths came without warning. One day, I had a normal phone conversation with our father. The next day, he had died of a heart attack next to the freeway on the way home from playing racquetball.

Living through these two deaths taught me that life can end for any of us at any time, for real. I try to appreciate all the time I have with the people I love most. For example, we weren't an "I love you" sort of family, so I never got the chance to tell my father I loved him. Since his death, I tell everyone I love them all the time. Seriously, everyone. The other day, I caught myself signing off after a two-hour conversation with a telephone customer service rep with "love you, Sahana, thanks for your time."

I mean…

But let's not pretend that I'm in full surrender. I'm still cavalier about all kinds of activities and connections and fully expect things to happen tomorrow the way my Google Calendar says they will. But the sense that this could be the last time does invite me to seize the day.

Recently, one of my brothers asked our other brother and me to drop everything and (learn to) play Mexican Train Dominoes (with Tequila) on a Tuesday night. Tuesday is typically my busiest work day, but this was a command performance. A game with my brothers? No contest. (To be clear, we're very competitive, so there is always a contest. The brother that's bringing the dominoes will probably win, and I will almost certainly lose, or die trying.)

And now that same brother announces he's coming to town early that (hot summer) day to swim in the river. So I wrote this section in my bathing suit.

A tool to try: HO'OPONOPONO HAWAIIAN FORGIVENESS PRAYER — A process to heal people or the separation between yourself and other people.

Type of tool: Knowing/Reality transforming

Best used for: Problems with people.

How to Use it: You can use this for whenever a place for healing presents itself in your life. If you have a resentment, a fear, a hurt, this simple prayer is transformative. Nowhere more so than in removing the barriers in your consciousness between life and death. Sometimes our fear of death (hence fear of life) is because we have so many regrets, resentments, and fears. This prayer can open us to complete forgiveness of ourselves and others and help us let go of the separation that exists between us and them and between life and death.

So just think of something about death that is hard for you, or simply think about death, or *why* you don't want to think about death. After identifying this place, with as much feeling as you can, say the below four statements:

- I'm sorry
- Please forgive me
- Thank you
- I love you

In doing this simple, powerful practice, it doesn't seem to matter whether I'm saying these words to myself, to my family, to God, or to life itself. Just say them (or listen to them, there are a million videos out there to find and enjoy) and let them flow over you whenever you are afraid of your death or the death of someone else.

Affirmation

I face death on death's terms so that I can face life on life's terms.

Reflection Questions

- What's stopping you from living fully?
- What are you dying to get out of?
- Who do you need to forgive to face life on life's terms?
- Who do you need to forgive to face death on death's terms?

CHAPTER 22

Know Your Feelings & Emotions

Every feeling is an arrow pointing to our healing.

—ADAPTATION OF THE BUDDHIST "PARABLE OF THE TWO ARROWS"

Why you must know your Feelings & Emotions

This section may run counter to the prevailing advice designed to help us improve our lives. This book, unlike many titles that appeal to the same people, is about *knowing,* not *feeling.* Every therapist and most self-help books will suggest that we feel our feelings to the fullest. They especially seem to love us to wallow in the bad ones. Whether it is anger, fear, or grief, we're advised to hang out in it, risk letting it overtake us. We are assured that letting ourselves feel our feelings will not hijack our whole day or life. Instead, we're encouraged to feel them fully and let the moment pass.

In my spiritual tradition, it has become increasingly important recently to avoid what's known as "spiritual bypass," whereby we skip directly to prayer or a spiritual solution when people are in pain. We're encouraged to take a beat and allow those feelings to surface.

Many people have now discovered that they have triggers and patterns that stem from traumatic childhood experiences, including everything from neglect to severe emotional, physical, and sexual abuse. These patterns can either be repressed or bring up extreme, lasting emotional effects.

Many speak openly about their inability to consistently "regulate" their emotions or feelings, finding themselves unable to work or function when "dysregulated."

At the same time, many of us and many who have experienced trauma or dysregulation, myself included, have used something, be it extra food, technology, alcohol, or sex (and constructively, we imagine, work and exercise) to avoid feeling whatever we might be feeling.

This section is a radical inquiry into a different question: Have we used whatever to avoid *feeling*? Or have we avoided *knowing?* Indeed, have we used *feelings* themselves as a way to avoid *knowing*? Are we so focused on what we feel, how we feel, and whether our emotions are "regulated or dysregulated" that we can't actually tell what we *know*?

Stream of Consciousness Inventory: Feelings & Emotions

Feeling is a lower harmonic of knowing.

— DR. DAIN HEER

To find out how powerful your Feelings & Emotions stream flows, rate each statement below on a scale of 1 to 5 according to how true/light that statement is for you. 5 indicates the statement is totally true/light, and 1 indicates that it is false/heavy. Add up your first five ratings to get your FLOW # and the second set of five ratings to get your GROW #. Subtract your GROW # from your FLOW # to get your current Feelings & Emotions Stream Power.

Assign a number to each statement below on how true/light the statement feels for you, 5 being the most true.

___ I know that 90% of all feelings I'm aware of are someone else's, not mine.
___ I don't have to take other people's feelings on board.
___ When I notice strong feelings, I can get curious and ask questions about them.
___ Feelings, when questioned, can point me to what I truly know.
___ I never blame my feelings and emotions for the conditions of my life.

For the five statements above, calculate your **FLOW #** _____

Feelings are a way to limit and negate your being, so every time you say "I feel," you're actually negating your being.

— DR. DAIN HEER

___ I don't seem to have a choice with feelings; when they come, they just take over.
___ I think that all feelings that I'm aware of are *my* feelings.
___ I can't really tell the difference between other people's feelings and my feelings.
___ I use so much (activity, food, drugs, you name it) that I can't even tell if I'm feeling a feeling, let alone whose it is.
___ Feeling "dysregulated" is often a reason I can't participate in some aspect of life.

For the five statements above, calculate your **GROW #** _____

Subtract your GROW # from your FLOW # to find out your KNOW # for your Feelings & Emotions.

FLOW - GROW = _______ KNOW

If your KNOW # is 17-25, congratulations, you're aware that you have emotions and feelings, and you allow yourself to feel them fully, and to point you in the direction of healing. You just might be a *Super Streamer* of Feelings & Emotions.

If your KNOW # is 8-16, you're aware you have feelings, and you can occasionally let yourself feel them but you try to keep it under control.

If your KNOW # is from less than 0 to 7, it could be an indication that you are avoiding feeling your feelings at all cost.

What I've Learned about Feelings & Emotions

Your body feels, but you as a being would perceive and know. Perceiving is no judgment, no ownership of whatever it is.

— DR. DAIN HEER

For a long time, I conflated feelings with *knowing*. In my family of origin, mom was the person allowed to have feelings. She alone could be visibly scared, sad, or mostly angry. She thrived in regret and fear; for her, pessimism was a strategy for living. If I expressed or named a feeling, she would tell me that I was wrong and that I didn't feel that. But what she was really denying was my *knowing*. To bring more order to my existence, I paid attention to her feelings, really *everyone's* feelings. Paying attention to other people's feelings covered up my ability to know.

Therapists focused a lot on feelings and tried to get me to feel mine or find mine. Maria Nemeth introduced me to the Buddhist concept of "the Monkey Mind." As I understood it, my mind could be cluttered with Monkey Mind, which I began to picture as my thoughts, dressed as monkeys swinging from fear to worry to doubt to fear again. I learned that what really separates successful people from unsuccessful people is not their feelings or their fear – everyone has fears, doubts, and worries–but the ability to tell the difference between Monkey Mind and that "still small voice".[47] Some Buddhist scholars suggest you can say to the Monkey Mind, "Thank you for sharing, nevertheless, I'm going to do X,Y or Z." (In other words, you don't have to listen.)

It wasn't until I stopped using eating, work, and other controlling behaviors, that I was able to detect what was underneath. For lack of a language to describe what I was detecting, I called it "feelings," but what if it was really *knowing*? As Dr. Dain Heer of Access Consciousness says, "Feeling is a lower harmonic of knowing." We are here to know, perceive, and receive so much from the part of us that is connected to all consciousness. We are hard-wired to receive it.

Yet, the focus on feelings, especially those of others, can obscure our ability to *know* what we know. That's the way it was for me. You may not have light or heavy addictions or dependencies covering up your *knowing*; you may have an opposite issue, feeling everything so intensely that you *can't* (or won't) know what you know.

Let's explore a cool, easy tool to get at the perception below the feelings.

47 1 Kings 19:11-12 KJV

What can you do to know your Feelings & Emotions?

A tool to try: WHAT FEELINGS AM I USING? — Question/Clearing to understand the core source of emotions: "What feelings am I using to create the yuck (WHATEVER THAT IS) that I am choosing?"

How, Why, Where & When to Use it: Any time you feel yuck or stuck, just say the question/clearing aloud, "What feelings am I using to create the yuck (go ahead and name it) that I am choosing?" whenever you're experiencing something really unpleasant, especially if it's that you're choosing a change or something new in your life. You may not perceive a connection between the feelings and the (non-changed or unpleasant) experience you're having, so that's why you're in doubt. These questions, like "what else is possible?" are not for you to answer. They are engineered to clear the "yuck or stuck" from your field so that your true intentions and *knowing* can bear fruit. At the end of it, you could say, "And everything that is, am I willing to destroy and uncreate?" If so, answer, "Yes!"

An example of applying this tool: Let's say I keep swearing off a food that I know doesn't serve me (either because it's unhealthy or I just can't seem to stop eating it once I start). Whether I'm experiencing any feelings at all is immaterial. I can still say,"How many feelings am I using to create the overeating I am choosing? And everything that is, am I willing to destroy and uncreate right now?" Keep saying it until you experience a shift.

Affirmation

I HAVE DESTROYED AND UNCREATED THE IMPELLED NEED TO USE FEELINGS TO CREATE THIS NEGATIVE CONDITION IN MY LIFE. I FREE MYSELF COMPLETELY OF THIS CONNECTION AND CLEAR MYSELF OF ALL THOUGHTS, BELIEFS, OPINIONS, AND CONCLUSIONS THAT HAVE DRIVEN THIS CONDITION.

Reflection Questions

- How much energy and attention are you paying to feelings rather than something else?
- Which feelings are yours and which are someone else's?
- What "yuck," if any, are you currently experiencing?
- How did the question work?

CHAPTER 23

So . . . What Do You Know?

To know yourself as the Being underneath the thinker, the stillness underneath the mental noise, the love and joy underneath the pain, is freedom, salvation, enlightenment.

— ECKHART TOLLE

You just had an opportunity to take 16 inventories on what and how you know what you know. And you learned 16 tools. You might now have a "KNOW" for every inventory you took. The only animal I found that has 16 legs is called a "Velvet Worm." So let's see what your Velvet Worm looks like:

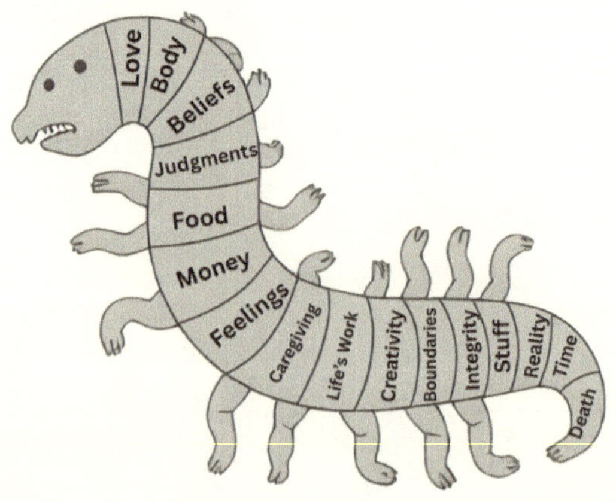

How Strong Are Your Legs of Knowing?

In the table below, you may make note of your Know # between -0 and 25 for any of the legs you inventoried.

Leg of Knowing	Know Number
Body & Healing	
Creativity	
Life's Work	
Judgments	
Food & Eating	
Love & Sex	
Money & Finance	
Stuff	
Time	
Integrity	
Boundaries	
Reality	
Caregiving	
Beliefs	
Death	
Feelings & Emotions	

Remember

- If your KNOW # is 17-25, you're in good shape
- If your KNOW # is 8-16 and this is an area that bothers you, you may want to work with the tool in that chapter to strengthen your knowing.
- If your KNOW # is between 0 and 7, and this is an area that bothers you, then you have a lot of room for improvement with the use of these tools.

SECTION

Living From Knowing

Every time she starts to question how she fits into it all, Ollie remembers that she is it, which removes the question.

— Z EGLOFF[48]

Pulling the Weeds of Consciousness

Although I strongly believe everyone can know, it's clear that not everyone *knows* what they know, and even fewer tune into it. Twenty years ago, when I started down a spiritual path, I didn't realize I had any inner wisdom to tune into. I acted out of habit and impulse. I routinely hurt myself and others with my choices and behavior. Years of therapy had not changed me or helped; they just provided more knowledge of why I was the way I was. It wasn't until I got into 12-step recovery from compulsive overeating and controlling behav-

48 *Timini* by Z Egloff

iors that I began to examine and *take responsibility for* my thoughts, beliefs, opinions, conclusions, and resentments. Throughout the writing of this book, I've struggled with the degree to which ridding one's consciousness of these weeds might be necessary to be able to accurately *know*.

Ultimately, only you can find your way to your *knowing,* but until I did the first "searching and fearless moral inventory" of myself, I thought I was a victim of the people around me. My first inventory showed me:

> I had good jobs, but not great ones, because my bosses didn't understand me, or my coworkers were getting privileges that were denied to me (it turned out I wasn't being the employee or coworker they deserved).
>
> I was living with an asshole who was really critical of me (and it turned out that "asshole" was me).
>
> My neighbors were controlling and vindictive (turned out that was me, too).

Unlike therapy,[49] the minute I stopped believing the lies I had been feeding myself, I began to change. Those (albeit unconscious) lies were like weeds that choked my mind, preventing it from hearing the profound wisdom inherent within me (and all people).

49 I have nothing against therapy but it didn't change my life and 12 steps did. Just sayin'.

Remember, You Always Have a Choice

This book is written for people who have a choice about whether to listen to or follow their inner wisdom, which is everyone. Many of us (maybe even most), regardless of our circumstances, feel like our choices are constrained. For millennia, people in the world have been too busy scrambling to find safety, food, water, and shelter to even consider anything but the most rudimentary choices as an unaffordable luxury. It may have seemed at the time that only the wealthy and powerful had any real choices. And it may seem like that today.

Yet, even in the most constricted times, such as the centuries of American chattel slavery, there were people who somehow escaped both their perceived extreme lack of choice and enslavement. Often that choice to escape resulted in death, torture, and an even worse existence, but occasionally it resulted in freedom. One such time was in 1862, when Robert Smalls led a group of friends and family out of slavery in South Carolina by commandeering a Confederate munitions ship and delivering it to the Union Army. He later became one of the first African American members of Congress, representing South Carolina during the period known as Reconstruction.

Or look at Viktor Frankl, the Austrian neurologist and psychiatrist who kept himself alive and sane inside a Nazi concentration camp by finding and writing *Man's Search for Meaning* inside his head. Talk about knowing what you know.

This is not to blame anyone for not perceiving that they have the choice to follow their inner knowing. It's just that history shows that even in some of the most extreme deprivation, we can access our inner *knowing,* which can lead the way to choice.

As a white, highly educated, affluent American born in the late 20th century, I can't pretend to understand what it's like to feel I don't have a choice. Even as a woman, almost all doors were open to me. Ten years before I chose to go to law school, only one in ten law students was a woman. By the time I went, half the students were female.

Yet, I notice that many relatively privileged people around me still perceive themselves to be stuck, certain that they can't find a love match, certain that the education or training they yearn for is out of reach for them, pretty sure that their body can never be healthier than it is. They perceive that they're alone, and without connection to a Higher Self that loves them unconditionally.

In English, we use the phrase "make up your mind" to mean "make a decision." Most of the time, however, by consulting anyone's wisdom but our own, we let others make up our minds for us. For thousands of years, people have sought guidance from the wise leaders of their cultures and religions. Most organized worldwide cultures and religions (but not all) encourage their followers to do just that: *follow*. The wisdom/rules of life have been decided. The elders/leaders know the rules. When we want to make decisions, we simply ask them, they tell us what to do, and then we do it.

Even if we live in a pluralistic culture and weren't brought up in a particular religion or structured sub-culture, we are unconsciously subject to the collective societal thoughts, beliefs, opinions, and conclusions about how we're supposed to be, what we're supposed to do, where we're supposed to live, and who and how we're supposed to love.

What a Day Looks Like Now, When You Start in Your Sacred Heart

We end this book as we began, except that now, instead of imagining how our days are, we can just begin to live them. As you start this day, perhaps you could try just one more special tool. I'd love for you to start your day sitting inside your Sacred Heart, a tool in the tool appendix that I did not tease out in the previous chapters.

By bathing in the unconditional love of Sacred Heart, you return to the place of *knowing*, power, and authority that is your divine birthright. Perhaps you can take all these qualities, tools, and thoughts with you in your day, to live them less alone. You may pause whenever you wish, to check out Light vs. Heavy, or the look at the Candle Flame, do some 2-Way Writing or simply mutter in traffic, "What else is possible?"

The day may not look a lot different than it did before the book, but perhaps it *feels* different. When things go wrong, perhaps you're releasing or allowing judgments to flow without using vital life energy to defend against them. Maybe you're even ending the day by harvesting gratitude from the day's most problematic twists and turns.

So as you go forth in the world, fiercely clutch the wisdom you have gained from this handbook: Your inner wisdom. Whether it's a book study, a class, a 12-step group, or joining an Ashram or spiritual community, find additional people to seat on the front row of your spiritual life who will remind you to look within, to listen, to see, to hear what's seeking you—those who will validate *your* truth as the truth, wherever possible.

What else is possible? How does it get even better than this?

Let me know!!!

Questions & Answers

Q: What if I can't tell light from heavy?

As discussed in "Why Don't We Know", it took me a couple of years of working with this tool to be able to relax into an awareness of space and light as a "yes" and an awareness of heaviness and stuckness as a "no." It was worth sticking with it, not just to be able to use this tool when I wanted to, but also to feel energy on the fly and realize, "Wow, this is light; I want to go toward it," or, "This is heavy, so it's not for me."

Q: I don't believe in God. Do I have to believe in God for this to work?

No. It would help, however, to come to believe that you are connected to more than just your own mind, that you have a Higher Self, or a Higher Intelligence into which you can tune. Try bringing to mind being out in nature or what it feels like to experience great art and fabulous music. How does that feel for you? That's the feeling of a connection we want. A connection with something more.

Q: Can I come up with my own way of finding my inner answers?

100%. The suggestions I'm making are really just what works for me and many others. Let me know what works for you. I'm genuinely interested. I'm sure there are as many ways of finding our own inner answers as there are answers.

Q: I didn't go to medical school. Why should I second-guess my doctors?

Doctors are part of divine intelligence. I listen to them carefully. But they are also human beings and fallible. What they're saying may be right for many, but is it light/right for me? So I listen and then I check it out with my own connection and do what's light for me. Or, sometimes I listen, and if it seems like there's no downside, I try whatever they suggest, even if I don't get a yes. Sometimes I disregard my own Divine Intelligence out of fear or a desire to please those around me. We are always free to choose. For example, I can imagine that if I had cancer, I might get a no on chemo or radiation, but I might decide to do it anyway.

Q: Does this mean I should never ask friends or family for advice or help on making decisions?

No. You are, of course, completely free to ask friends and family for help. However, please proceed with caution. Not only do our friends and family, however loving and well-meaning, have their own agendas and needs, but also the mere act of asking them can produce stress for them or give them the idea that they are now partners in a decision that is ours to make. That's totally fine, like in the case of a committed partnership, many decisions might be something to make together. However, I've been married for decades, and I've learned that it's better for me to start with my own discernment before I broach the subject with my partner. At that point, they can begin their own discernment process. *then* we can come together to discuss what it means for us as a couple.

Q: What if I'm an addict in 12-step recovery? As it says in the ("Big Book" of) Alcoholics Anonymous, it's suggested that we check things out from other people and not go around telling ourselves, our "Higher Power" told us to do this.

Do what your sponsor suggests. Talk it over with them. Ask them and others in your recovery circles how they handle this. Note that while the "Big Book" also says "What used to be the hunch or the occasional inspiration gradually becomes a working part of the mind" and "...we find that our thinking will, as time passes, be more and more on the plane of inspiration. We come to rely upon it."

Q: In my tradition, when we turn for "higher" wisdom, it is to God and not onto a part of ourselves. Isn't what you're suggesting blasphemous?

A: There is no doubt some religions and periods of time that would have burned me at the stake for suggesting this. That's certainly part of what brought Joan of Arc down. I'm truly hoping that we no longer live in those times. However, in *The Universal Christ*, contemporary Catholic priest Richard Rohr dedicates an entire book to explaining and interpreting the Christian Gospel, persuading us that Christ is not a person or Jesus's last name. Jesus came to teach us that we all carry and can access the Christ within us in what some would call our Sacred Heart.

Q: In my tradition, we don't see a separation between ourselves and God (or Higher Wisdom). We pray from God, not to God. Isn't the concept of conscious contact between ourselves and a "Higher Self" sort of engaging in "separation"?

A: In a word, no. It's not. In my view, we are proceeding from the understanding that Spirit is everything in the known and unknown worlds and is living out its perfect life as us. Therefore, there is a part of us that has access to the infinite knowing of Spirit as us.

Q: How do I remember to use these tools?

One great way might be to choose a friend to serve as an accountability partner. Ask if you can text them when you're going to check in with yourself. See if they want to do the same. You don't have to share the results of your inquiry, but you can if you choose to. Or peg it to any other habit (what that "habit guy" calls "Stacking"). For example, after your morning pee or tea, do morning check-ins, or after you brush your teeth, do your nightly check-ins.

Q: Who the heck are you to tell me who to listen to or not?

No one. I'm just this person who is excited about self-inquiry and has thought about it. Feel free to disregard.

Q: What's a low-stakes way to practice these tools?

A: Oh, so glad you asked, I almost forgot. Use your basic tools (Light vs. Heavy or Candle Flame) on everything (just to see what happens). Instead of using navigation, consider using your tools. Choose a time, place, or guest for lunch by using them. Just to practice. When you don't really care how it comes out.

But also, something like Sudoku is a great way to build your belief. In Sudoku, there's one right and nine wrong numbers to put in every single square. The harder the puzzle, the less likely you are to be able to decide analytically on the number, so I've found it's a fun way to test the tool. Narrow it down to three numbers analytically and then feel into the tools, which is the lightest or generates the strongest flame?

Q: Why didn't you find the handbook before?

Maybe you didn't find it before because I didn't write it before or maybe it's because the other books told you that it was something outside of yourself that you were connecting with. Maybe because it just wasn't yet time.

Q: What if everyone knew what they knew?

I'm writing this book in a time of great division in my country. I can't help wondering what this country and the world would be like if everyone *knew* what they *knew*. Would this be closer to looking and feeling like a world that works for everyone?

It might be true that helping everyone *know* more about what they *know* could change the world; maybe that's even one of the reasons I wrote this book.

Ultimately, the only knowing I can ensure is my own.

The Tools Appendix

Clearing the Way for Knowing Tools

The following tools are not to *know* but to make it easier to *know*. One thing I've struggled with throughout the writing of this book is the degree to which ridding one's consciousness of old beliefs, fears, resentments, shame, and guilt might be necessary to accurately hear one's inner wisdom.

As I said earlier, when I started down a spiritual path, I didn't realize I had inner wisdom to dial into. I acted out of habit and impulse. I routinely hurt myself and others with my choices and behavior. It wasn't until I got into 12-step recovery from compulsive overeating and controlling that I began to examine and *take responsibility* for my thoughts, beliefs, opinions, conclusions, and resentments.

Due to my experience, while I can say with certainty that we all can access inner wisdom, I cannot be sure that one can access it without doing the kind of work I've done. In addition to the therapy,[50] and 12-step work, as a Science of Mind[51] minister, I now plant many seeds to change my experience of reality. I find that the

---

50 Again, I have nothing against therapy but it didn't change my life.

51 Centers for Spiritual Living

clearer my consciousness, the sweeter the fruit. It gets worse; like any good garden, the bed of my mind requires constant tending. Hence, below, I present my favorite tools for clearing my mind.

TOOL: The 12 Steps

Purpose: To recover from addiction.

How to use it: Figure out the addiction you *might* have, and then look it up on the internet and go to a meeting of the anonymous fellowship that fits your problem.[52] If you want what I have found, ask a "sponsor" to lead you through the 12 steps and finish all 12 steps as quickly as possible.

Best used for: recovery from addiction and co-addiction

Type of tool: Knowing/Reality transforming

Tool: Existential Kink Meditation[53]

Purpose: To find out how you're "getting off on" all the things you think you hate.

How to use it:

> Get yourself into a relaxed state for 15 minutes.
> Identify a situation in your life that your conscious mind, your ego, does not like.
> Identify exactly what feelings and emotions you associate with this situation.

52 There are so many 12-step fellowships, you won't believe it. Not only are there fellowships such as Alcoholics Anonymous and Narcotics Anonymous, there are fellowships for compulsive overeating, workaholism, cluttering, debting, gambling, codependence and so forth. If you think that YOU aren't the addict but that you are bothered by someone else's using there are also 12-step fellowships for what is called co-addiction, starting with Al-Anon Family Groups for friends and family members of alcoholics, and others.

53 From chapter 3 of *Existential Kink* by Carolyn Elliott

Gently allow yourself to get in touch with the part of yourself that actually, passionately enjoys the feelings and emotions associated with your "don't like" situation.

Experiment with playfully saying the following EK statements to yourself:

"I'm willing to stop pretending I don't enjoy XYZ tremendously."

or "I'm willing to allow myself to know about my secret, weird pleasure in XYZ."

or "It's okay for me to feel my forbidden, wicked enjoyment of XYZ without having to judge it negatively or disown it."

You can also experiment with saying EK statements such as these:

"I'm totally allowed to have this weird enjoyment of XYZ. I don't need to shame it, I don't need to regret it, I don't need to deny it." "I'm allowed to want exactly what I want, even if it's 'bad' or 'wrong' or 'destructive.'"

Get on the side of your shadow (your previously unconscious sense of desire/curiosity/enjoyment) and deliberately, consciously, humbly allow yourself to receive, feel big gratitude for, and get off on the situation your unconscious so brilliantly created.

Best used for: Anytime a pattern is not shifting through other means

Similar to: "Reclaiming Reality" tool explored in "Know Your Reality"

Type of tool: Knowing (at least that you get off on it)/Reality transforming

Tool: Radical Forgiveness[54]

Purpose: Traditional forgiveness is "Something went terribly wrong but I'm going to forgive anyway." The purpose of radical forgiveness to grasp how, at the level of the soul, "nothing went wrong."

Best used for: Persistent resentments, judgment, or anger toward a given person or situation that just don't seem to shift.

How to use it: Download and fill out the Radical Forgiveness Worksheet https://www.soundstrue.com/pages/radicalforgiveness

Read it to a trusted person. Burn it afterwards or tear it into pieces and throw them away.

Similar to: Working the first nine steps of the 12-steps on something all in one swoop.

Type of tool: Knowing/Reality transforming

For more information: www.radicalforgiveness.org. You can work with a trained Radical Forgiveness coach or read the book *Radical Forgiveness* by Colin Tipping.

54 For more information, visit www.radicalforgiveness.org. You can work with a trained Radical Forgiveness coach or read the book *Radical Forgiveness* by Colin Tipping.

Tool: Pull-Judgment From[55]

Purpose: Allows you to "receive" the judgment and energy, rather than "resist and defend." The act of doing so seems to invite judgment from the world, which actually enriches us quite literally. I was told that for every judgment I pull, I would receive $1,000 more in income per year. And that has occurred.

Best used for: Whenever you are feeling judged by someone or a group of "someones" (entire family, friends, colleagues, staff, congregants, political parties) you can "pull" (which really means stop defending against) judgment from them.

How to use it: The super easy way is whenever you feel judged, say aloud three times:

> "Pull judgment from ____(NAME)____".

To explain what it means in the language of affirmative prayer, we might say:

> "I am an infinite being of light and love. Nothing can hurt me because nothing sticks to me. Therefore, I cease all defending or bracing myself against judgment. I lower all barriers. I cease using any of my vital life force to defend. I allow and invite all judgments from _______ to come to me, to bring me energy, wealth, vitality, and joy, and to flow right through me and return to the original source of light and love (or to Mother Earth to be composted)."

55 Another Access Consciousness tool

I've had incredible experiences where, within an hour of saying "pull judgment from _____," the person apologizes to me not just for whatever they were judging me for at the moment, but for a whole host of things. I've had people mail me checks and apologies. You name it.

Type of tool: Reality transforming

Tool: New Conclusion[56]

Purpose: Engages us to change the focus of our attention to gather evidence for a *new* conclusion (or belief, if you will) mostly about someone else.

Best used for: The perfect time to use it is when you're feeling really frustrated with someone and wish they would change and have gathered a lot of evidence to support your conclusions about that person. This works especially well with beliefs about the people around us, but it can work with something just to do with yourself.

How to use it: First, identify a firm belief (that plagues you) for which you've gathered evidence: Here's one I periodically have:

My neighbor is resentful and controlling.

There's nothing I can do about that belief. I've gathered mental file cabinets full of evidence that my neighbor is resentful and angry, all of which I would be happy to recite to prove to them, you, or myself that I'm right. So what can I do?

---

56 From Maria Nemeth *Mastering Life's Energies*

Craft a new conclusion for which I am willing to gather evidence. I'm tired of them showing up that way. I'm tired of seeing these neighbors as resentful and angry. I'm tired of just hoping they will move. So, I try gathering evidence for a *new* conclusion: *my neighbor is loving and accepting.*

Begin to gather evidence for this conclusion. This does not seem true to me, but I'm just going to pretend that I'm a spiritual detective and that I have a new client who's paying me to spy on this neighbor and gather evidence to support this conclusion.

This evidence affects how I show up. As I gather this evidence for the new conclusion (my neighbor is loving and accepting), it affects how I show up around them (even if I'm not interacting with them, it affects me energetically, how and whether I gossip or even *want* to gossip about them to my husband or others, etc.)

Which affects how they *show up.* As I gather this new evidence, it begins to shift my perspective on how I think and how I show up (even just energetically) with them. This, in turn, can affect how *they* show up with me and my community.
This strengthens my new conclusion and generates additional evidence for that conclusion.
And so it continues

Type of tool: Reality transforming

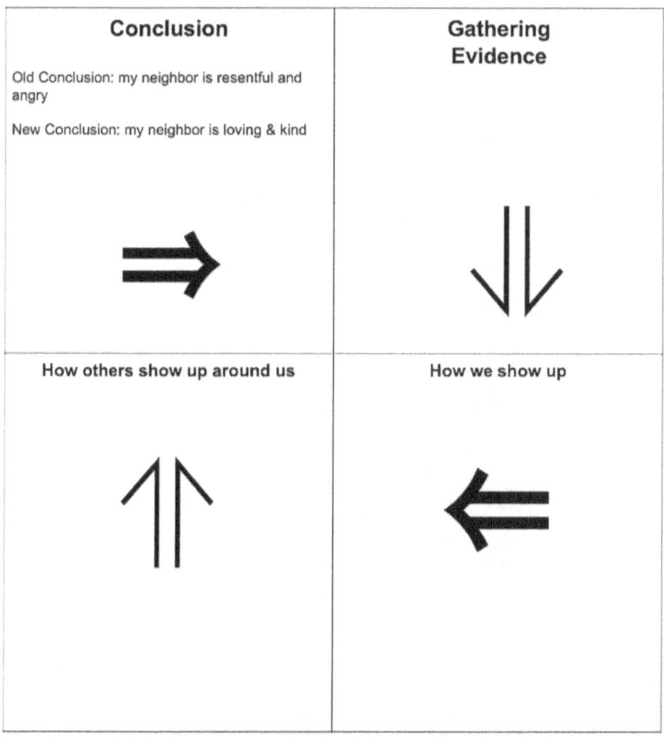

From Mastering Life's Energies by Maria Nemeth, P. 103

Tool: The Four Questions[57]

Purpose: To examine a judgment or thought about someone or something to see if it's really true.

Best used for: Persistent resentments, especially an idea that someone else *should* or *should not* do something.

57 Aka Byron Katie's "The Work"

How to use it:

Download the "Judge Your Neighbor Worksheet" https://share.google/nOgpmt15c0hRZnBHh

Fill it out and read it to someone else. (Preferably someone who is familiar with "The Work.")

Type of tool: Knowing/Reality transforming

Tool: Emotional Freedom Technique: EFT (aka "tapping")[58]

Purpose: Emotional regulation or clearing emotional (and perhaps neural) pathways that make it hard to focus, function, or regulate.

Best used for: Any emotional upset that is making it hard or impossible to function/tune into inner knowing.

How to use it: Identify what you're upset about. Rate on a scale of 1 to 10 how upset you feel. Create a statement that acknowledges the upset yet grounds you where you want to be, like "Even though I'm angry at my sister, I completely love and accept myself."

Tap on each point in this order as you say that statement over and over:

- Tap repeatedly on the edge of your palm below your little finger.
- Tap on the top, center of your head.
- Tap on the inside edge of one eyebrow.

58 For more information, checkout The Tapping Solution/EFT https://share.google/xYNfoOrOYyLCnPK4t or numerous videos

- Tap next to the outside edge of one eye.
- Tap on the bone underneath one eye.
- Tap between your nose and your upper lip.
- Tap between your lower lip and your chin.
- Tap beneath one collarbone (find the notch beneath the inside edge of the collarbone).
- Tap under one armpit (about 4 inches below the armpit).

Take a moment to reassess your feelings about the issue.
Repeat the steps if needed.
Tap until you can assign a lower number to your issue, or until you feel better.

Type of tool: Reality transforming

Top How to Know Tools

Tool: Light vs. Heavy

Purpose: Determine whether a choice is light or heavy energetically for you.

Best used for: Day-to-day, little and big choices, everything. Your basic *know* tool.

How to use it: This one can be used on practically anything and is the strongest tool in the book for that reason. It is a decision-making tool. It is carried with you everywhere. It comes from Access Consciousness. The basics of it are whatever the choice is, if you ask yourself, "What will my life feel like in five years if I do this thing?" And then feel into it. Does it feel light and expansive, or does it feel heavy and constricted? Then ask, how does it feel if I don't do it or do something else? Light and expansive is a yes. Heavy and constricted is a no.

Also described (and used) in: "How to Use this Book", and throughout "Getting to Know You"

Type of tool: Know

Tool: Candle flame

Purpose: Determine whether a choice makes your internal candle flame burn brighter or flicker and go out

Best used for: Day-to-day, little and big choices, everything. If Light vs. Heavy doesn't work, this could be your basic *know* tool

How to use it: Picture a candle burning bright in your chest. Now, if you take choice A, what happens to the candle? If you take choice B, what happens to the candle? Generally, if the candle burns brighter and stronger, that's a yes; if it burns weaker and flickers or goes out, that's a no.

Also described (and used) in: "How to Use this Book: Your Basic Tool for Knowing", and throughout "Getting to Know You and Know Your Food & Eating"

Type of tool: Know

Other Key Know Tools

Tool: Coincidence/Signs

Purpose: Tracking, noticing, and paying attention to synchronicities in your life as signposts showing you which way to go.

Best used for: Strong spiritual evidence pointing the way at a fork in the road of your life: work, relationships, geographic moves.

How to use it: Track coincidences in a journal. Note anything that appears to be a coincidence. The less probable the coincidence, the more difficult it is to see it as anything but a sign; the more we circle it, star it, and tease it out to remember. Once we notice coincidences, we can follow them to our good.

Also described (and used) in: "Know Your Life's Work"

Type of tool: Know

Tool: 2-Way Writing

Purpose: Brings you into dialogue with your Higher Self, your inner knowing.

Best used for: Any KWYK tool cultivates *knowing,* but this one cultivates the relationship between your ego self and your Higher Self.

How to use it: Pen or paper, or on a computer, your choice. Write to your Higher Self (call them what you can/do, doesn't matter what, I call mine "Spirit Team"). Then have them write back to you. Here's a sample:

Start with a greeting to your Higher Self:

> Dear Spirit Team, I love you. How are you?

Higher Self replies (I'll use italics for what they say back to me, which is what I do when I capture it on a keyboard):

> *Hi, Sara. We love you too. We are happy to hear from you as always.*
> I'm sorry it's been so long since I've written. I have been absorbed in my own head. I've been trying to fix this on my own. I need your help.

They might add:

> *We have watched you, Sara. We love you. We welcome your questions at any time. We admire you. We do not experience time passing. So it is not a "wait" as you might say.*
> Okay, so here's what's up for me today. I am scared and I don't know what to do. Here's the situation. And here's a question I have.

And then of course I pour my heart out. Everything that I'm afraid of, worried about, trying to decide, all of it, anything at all that I need to say. There's no reason to censor myself, but take whatever precautions for your privacy that you need.

And then I ask a question. Because God (or a Spirit Team) is literally infinitely patient, I've found that it's not like talking to a close friend, family member, or even a therapist, where they might feel empowered to jump right in with answers, ideas, or advice. Spiritual etiquette requires that we ask for help. This is helpful to me because taking the time to formulate my real questions can be the key to getting answers. Until I know what I'm really asking, I may be unable to receive the answers I need.

Sometimes I type out a list of possible things I'm deciding between (kind of like the pieces of paper exercise, but not double-blind) and just hover my finger over each one, asking in my head, "What do you think of this?" etc. Sometimes that just gives me a light or heavy feeling, or sometimes words from the team spring to my fingers. Whatever it is, I write it down.

Other people write longhand in a journal or notebook. Many advise using their dominant hand for their own (self/ego) questions and then responding to the questions using their non-dominant hand. For most of us, it's hard to write with our non-dominant hand, so it only produces a couple of barely legible words.

When I try it this way (longhand/switching hands), I usually attempt to copy the words from my Higher Self/Higher Power with my right hand, and perhaps augment/capture the thought while it's still available to me mentally/emotionally.

There's a decades-old Alcoholics Anonymous adjacent practice of "two-way prayer" with a whole script of phrases to utter to set the stage for the conversation and things to ask one's higher self. It's pretty cool too. A quick internet search will provide a delicious spread of options to learn or practice this tool.

Also described (and used) in: "Know Your Creativity"

Type of tool: Know/Reality Transforming

Tool: Havingness Gauge

Purpose: A quick and easy mental picture of the degree to which we're willing to have what we say we want.

Best used for: You claim to want a vibrant democracy, the perfect partner, a great job, a beautiful home, a healthy body, but if you never see that/perceive that in reality, could your degree of "havingness" be part of the issue? Check the gauge.

How to use it: In your mind's eye, picture an old-fashioned gas gauge on the deck of your car with 0% on the left and 100% on the right. That's your "Havingness Gauge."[59] Think of something you have wanted for a while, but hasn't shown up yet. Let's say it's a high-paying job (whatever that means to you). Ask the Gauge to what degree you are willing to "have" (rather than just "want") a high-paying job. What happens on the gauge? Does it go to 30% havingness? 70%? 100% wherever it is, that's the degree to which you are willing to have it (or not).

Also described (and used) in: "Know Your Love & Sex Life"

Type of tool: Know/Reality Transforming

59 A tool I learned from the Berkeley Psychic Institute

Tool: Double-Blind Paper Test[60]

Purpose: A double-blind way to discern light or heavy for multiple competing choices.

How to use it: Say I've budgeted for a 1-week trip to an exotic world destination and I'm trying to decide between 4 possible locations. Cut 4 pieces of paper to be the same shape and size. Write each location on one side and on the other side write "1," "2," "3", "4" (doesn't matter which one has which number, and doesn't have to be a number, could be a letter or an animal sticker or a color, don't overthink it and DON'T note which destination has which code on the other side!) Turn them all over so that the destination (or options you're deciding amongst) are all facing down. Move them all around so that there's no particular order to them. Then put your hand over each piece of paper and feel whether it feels light or heavy (or, if you prefer, observe the candle flame burning brighter or flickering and threatening to go out). In a separate place, note on a scale of 1 to 5 how light it feels, with 5 being the lightest or perhaps the brightest flame. As you see the code in your notes, again feel into it and make note of it.

Determine which of all the options is the lightest. Note that you are now double or maybe triple blind on this, so that it's not just about your conscious mind making the decision.

Turn over the papers and see which option felt the most expansive for you without knowing how expensive it is. Do the whole thing again with different papers if you feel it's not credible. Sometimes the second try is the most convincing.

60 I learned this from Katie Rubin who might have learned it from Access Consciousness

Best used for: You have multiple competing possibilities for your time, and you are stuck in your head about it and can't trust yourself enough to compare each one without putting your finger on the scale of your consciousness.

Type of tool: Know

Also described in: "Know Your Money & Finances"

Tool: What Feelings Am I Using?

Purpose: Using a question to determine where feelings are getting in the way of a choice.

How to use it: Say the question/clearing aloud:

> What feelings am I using to create the yuck (WHATEVER THAT IS–Name it) that I am choosing?"
> And everything that is, am I willing to destroy and uncreate it?
> Yes!

You may not perceive a connection between the feelings and the (nonchanged or unpleasant) experience that you're having, so that's why you're in the question. These questions, like "What else is possible?", are not for you to answer. They are engineered to clear what Dr. Dain would call "yuck, stuck & wtf" from your field so that your true intentions and *knowing* can bear fruit. At the end of it, you could say, "And everything that is, am I willing to destroy and uncreate?" If so, answer, "Yes!"

Best used for: Whenever you're experiencing something really unpleasant, especially when you're considering a change or something new in your life, but it's not feeling good.

Type of tool: Know/Reality Transforming

Also described (and used) in: "Know Your Feelings & Emotions"

Tool: Gates to the Sacred Yes

Purpose: Four simple questions to take you from Sacred No (your resting place) to Sacred Yes.

How to use it: Whenever you're asked to do something, your first response can be, "Let me reflect on it and get back to you." Then sit quietly and ask yourself these questions. You can write the answers if that helps.

> Gate 1: Does it absolutely need to be done by someone?
>
> Gate 2: Does it absolutely need to be done now (as opposed to the future)?
>
> Gate 3: Does it absolutely need to be done by me?
>
> Gate 4: Can I do it with clarity, focus, ease, grace and most of all, joy?
>
> Once all four gates are passed, you are at Sacred Yes.

Best used for: Some of us have our default answer as "yes'. No matter what we're asked, we say it. If you've been a default no, switching to this strategy can flip the switch to a life well lived (as Shonda Rhimes writes in her book *My Year of Yes: How to Dance it Out, Stand in the*

Sun and Be Your Own Person). But when we say yes mindlessly and reflexively, or worse, from guilt and codependence, it can lead to burnout and illness.

Type of tool: Know

Also described (and used) in: "Know Your Time"

Tool: What Else Is Possible?[61]

Purpose: Ask for help from our Higher Self and to stir up new possibilities when we don't see any good choices.

How to use it: Ask aloud, "What else is possible?" You can whisper it or say it under your breath if you feel embarrassed, but saying it aloud actually goes over really well in *most* circumstances.

Best used for: Anytime you're feeling stuck or like there are no good options. That can be a profound existential crisis or despair, or it can occur in mundane situations, such as being stuck in traffic. Just asking this question aloud shifts us from being solely interested in what we think are the parameters of the possible to accessing the part of us that is connected to the unlimited. And then, having said that, our only job is to get curious and pay attention to what thoughts, signs, and occurrences happen that may bring a "new" thought or a "new" possibility to our consciousness.

Type of tool: Know/Reality Transforming

Also described (and used) in: "See Know Your Stuff"

61 Access Consciousness tool – www.accessconsciousness.com

Tool: Standards of Integrity Inventory

Purpose: Determine your standards of integrity.

How to use it: Make three columns. In the first column, list five people that you admire, living or dead, known to you or famous. The next column is all the qualities that you admire about that particular person. In the third column, pull out all the qualities that you listed for each person and put a check mark next to each quality that you admire in that person.

Best used for: If you're embarking on any inventory where you might be looking predominantly at where you're out of alignment, use this inventory to light your way and show who you really are.

Type of tool: Know

Also described in: "Know Your Integrity"

Tool: Body Dialogue

Purpose: Speaking and listening to your body or a body part to discern what it really needs.

How to use it: Listening to your body can be as simple as this: Sit with a journal or voice recorder handy and your hand (if possible) on the part of the body in discomfort, or that you associate with the discomfort, and say aloud, "What are you trying to tell me?" "What wisdom do you have for me"? and then making note of it.

Best used for: Any time you have a persistent physical ailment that your usual remedies don't shift.

Type of tool: Know/Reality Transforming

Also described (and used) in: "Know Your Body & Health"

Tool: Best Thing You Believe

Purpose: Zero in on the beliefs that serve you rather than those that don't.

How to use it: Take a given area where you want to manifest or change something.

Write a list of all the things you believe about your ability to manifest or change that something. Don't try to distinguish whether those beliefs are *useful* or not. Just make a list.

Move your finger down the list and, using the Light vs. Heavy or the Candle Flame tool, dial into which feels the lightest (or generates the strongest candle flame) on the list for you to focus on. The question you're asking yourself is really, what is the best (or most useful) belief you have on this question?

Which belief stands out? Let's say it was "somehow the name of the right person will come to me." Now *that's* the belief you focus your prayers, your intentions, and your *curiosity* on. (see "Know Your Beliefs" for an example)

Best used for: You have a goal. You don't know where to start. Examine your beliefs to find the ones that are most useful. Then focus on those.

Type of tool: Know/Reality Transforming

Also described (and used) in: "Know Your Beliefs"

Tool: "You May Be Right"

Purpose: To have something to say when you don't know what to say and to open up new ideas.

How to use it: You can just say, "You may be right" (or its cousin, "Can you believe it?!') when someone says something you profoundly disagree with but don't want to argue about. You can also use the chart in "Know Your Boundaries" as a way to generate a variety of phrases and actions to use with difficult people.

Best used for: When you repeatedly interact with a specific person (often a family member, but sometimes a coworker or someone else) and you find yourself allowing them to harm you in various ways, this is a tool you can use to access your inner wisdom and come up with new ideas.

Type of tool: Know/Reality Transforming

Also described (and used) in: "Know Your Boundaries"

Tool: Let Them Know What They Know

Purpose: So you can focus on knowing what *you* know and let others focus on knowing what they know.

How to use it: The main thing to "do" is not to do. As long as it will not harm someone else, or as the harm to themselves is not truly our responsibility, let our children, our parents, and those we are caring for know what they know and do what they do no matter how stupid or weird or wasteful it seems. If they don't ask us for help, let them be and do what they're being and doing.

Best used for: Letting go of trying to control others by letting them know what they know is helpful in any aspect of a relationship, but particularly when it comes to parenting children or parents.[62]

Type of tool: Know/Reality Transforming

Also described (and used) in: "Know Your Caregiving"

Tool: Interesting Point of View

Purpose: To clear judgments we have of others.

How to use it: To clear judgments we have of others, say aloud "Interesting point of view, I have that point of view" three times.

Best used for: When you catch yourself judging others. The concept is that every judgment we have of others is something that is inherently in us, not them. In essence, "Interesting point of view, I have that point of view" means I replace *judgment* of the person I'm judging's actions and words with *curiosity* about their point of view. More than that, it means I experiment with owning the very point of view that I have been judging.

Type of tool: Know/Reality Transforming

Also described (and used) in: "Know Your Judgments"

---

62 If you consistently find that you cannot refrain from focusing on or trying to contol the behavior of people who are not children under 10 and that bothers you, consider visiting Al-Anon Family Groups https://al-anon.org/ to learn more tools.

Tool: Reclaiming Reality

Purpose: Reclaim (your real) Reality by telling your apparent reality/story and reclaiming your power from it.

How to use it: Use the tool as outlined in "Know Your Reality".

Best used for: Use this powerful tool when you find yourself feeling victimized or powerless in what you perceive to be "the reality."

Type of tool: Know/Reality Transforming

Also described (and used) in: "Know Your Reality"

Tool: Visioning Meditation

Purpose: To catch what is coming next in your life or an area of your life.

How to use it: Sit quietly with a notebook in hand. Breathe. Ask yourself (or others; this is often done in a group):

> *What is the highest vision for my (life, health, relationship, work, group, project, etc.)?*
> (pause and take time to listen or see–capture any words, colors, images, thoughts that come to you, no matter how random or unconnected they may seem)
>
> *What must I release for me to allow this vision to emerge?*
> (pause again as above)
>
> *What must I embrace to support the highest unfolding of this vision?* (pause)

Is there anything else about this vision that is ready to be revealed in this moment? (pause)

Give thanks for what you have been shown.

Do this again several times over the course of days, weeks, or months. Look for external reflections of what you have been shown as signposts leading you toward your vision.

Best used for: You want a new job, a new relationship, a dream vacation, or to help build or create something wonderful, a new business, or a nongovernmental organization.

Type of tool: Know/Reality Transforming

For more information: *Life Visioning: A Transformative Process for Activating Your Unique Gifts and Highest Potential* by Michael Beckwith.

Tool: Gratitude List

Purpose: To realize/know that there is a part of you that is actually grateful for most of your life, even the parts that don't seem good.

How to use it:

Every day, either at the beginning or the end of the day (I do it at the end), write a quick list of 20 things you're grateful for, specific or unique to that very day. So not "my spouse, my cat, my home" every day, but more like something particular to that day for my spouse, my cat, or my home.

Whatever's the worst thing that happened that day, explore that for gratitude. If I got stuck next to the road with a flat tire for hours, maybe I could feel grateful that I:

1. Had a towing service
2. Had air conditioning
3. Had a cell phone
4. Had some time to think/vision/know what I know

And so on.

I do this gratitude practice almost every single evening (I'm too tired to do it like four times a year) before I fall asleep. It takes me about three minutes to do it because I keep my focus throughout the day on what to be grateful for. The reason it's a *know* tool rather than just a change of consciousness tool is that it makes me realize that this is the actual truth. Spirit is living out its life as me and enjoys *all* of it. I have an opportunity to simply dial into it and see and feel and know what Spirit *as me* sees and feels and knows.

Best used for: Daily spiritual Prosac. This technique can literally change my attitude and my feelings by choosing to be grateful for virtually everything.

Type of tool: Knowing/Reality transforming

Tool: Your Sacred Heart

Purpose: Dropping into your Sacred Heart.

Best used for: Preparing the way to know.

How to use it: In the nonfiction book, *Love Without End: Jesus Speaks,* author and painter Glenda Green reports that Jesus came to her in the 1990s and asked her to paint His portrait. During this time they had numerous conversations, which she transcribes. She says that Jesus told her that each of us has within us a Sacred Heart, which we can enter and be safe from all harm and receive all wisdom that is available to us. This sitting Jesus says that the Lord's Prayer is the key to entering the Sacred Heart. And he describes precisely where the Sacred Heart lives in the body.

> (The easiest way to enter is to) quiet your mind through surrender and resolve, allowing your attention to become like a pebble cast into a great, still *lake*. And then float away in the stillness and vacuity until you come to rest.
>
> Sit for at least 10 minutes in the unconditional love of this heart, allowing it to restore to you your ability to know and know that you know.

Type of tool: Knowing/Reality transforming

Tool: Muscle-Testing

Purpose: Muscle-testing is a way of using the body's innate wisdom to see whether something is a yes or a no.

How to use: The most basic kind requires two people:

> Hold your arm out at shoulder level.
> First, have someone ask you a yes or no question that you know the answer to, like, "Is your name ________?"
>
> ...and push down on your arm when you answer.
> If the arm is hard to push down, it's a yes;
> if it's easy, like you can barely keep it up, it's a no.
> Then keep having them ask you questions (you may want to prepare them in advance).
>
> It requires a second person to do it right, which is a limitation in some ways, but for many, that might add to their trust in the process. You could trade muscle testing with someone. While professionals use it, you don't have to be a professional to use it.

Best used for: Because it's a test right on the body, many, including alternative medicine doctors, use muscle testing to discern what supplements, foods, or techniques serve the body. I see an applied kinesiologist chiropractor. Applied kinesiology "uses a technique of diagnosing health problems by testing for weakness in muscles and observing posture, strength, and range of motion. Those who use this technique believe a relationship exists between weakness in a muscle and a corresponding organ."[63]

Type of tool: Know

Tool: Dream Journal

Purpose: To use your dreams, gateway to the unconscious, to guide your waking life.

How to use it: There are tons of resources out there about interpreting dreams and catching dreams, so I'm not going to try to replicate that, but get straight to the basics. Even if you think you "don't dream" or "can't remember them," experiment by putting a dream journal and pen next to your bed with the intention of catching any fragments of dreams (however vague) when you wake. Whether you wake in the middle of the night or in the morning, if you can capture anything at all, write it down in the journal.

Make note especially of any feelings you remember from the dream. What's important is not whether the knight was white or talking backwards or forwards. It's how you felt about it.

Then, in interpretation, the essential truth is that you look at every part of the dream as yourself. You are the white knight, you are the red queen, you are Alice, you are the caterpillar. Yes, you could follow some dream interpretation book to look up what each of those means, but remember, this is about *your* knowing, not some book's idea of what these things mean.

Then, as you did with the Coincidences, and Visioning Medita-

63 learn.org

tion tools, look for signs and signals in the "real world" that match what you've been shown. These are clues on your journey.

Best used for: All the other tools for knowing are primarily focused on your conscious mind, trying to contact your Higher Self, the part of you that *knows* and knows that it knows. This tool is a form of communication *from* your unconscious mind to your conscious mind. I have found that by paying attention to my dreams, I remember them and they provide me with information I wouldn't otherwise have about the focus of my unconscious mind.

Type of tool: Knowing

Other Tools That Help

Tool: Letter From Your Future Self

Purpose: A letter you write to yourself from your future self. It reveals how your life will unfold in various aspects of your life.

Best used for: Making decisions and manifesting in any area, but especially career or relationships. Get underneath the ideas you have in your head and into how you really want to feel.

How to use it: Use the following template to create your own letter. Once you create it, have it handy so you can read it to yourself every day.

Letter from Your Future Self

Dated: __________, 20__ (6 months from today or more)

Dear (Your Name),

(You would not believe how great my life is and how wonderful it is to be alive now. I want to tell you about it.)

(Choose from these categories and edit the sample feelings below to fit your vision of your life.)

In my relationships & family:

(I feel respected and loved and cherished by my family, friends, and life partner. I feel creative and passionate. I feel abundant and free.)

In my body:

(I feel energetic and alive. I love life and it loves me.)

In my dwelling or home:

(I feel happy, secure, and joyful in my home. It is beautiful and serene…)

In my school/creativity/work:

(I am creative and inspired. I feel respected, cherished, and amply compensated. I make a difference in the world...)

In my finances:

(I feel stress-free and I have choices. I choose what I want to do by what it is, not what it costs.)

Love,

Your name

Type of tool: Knowing/Reality transforming

Tool: Feelings & Needs Checklists[64]

Purpose: To identify and communicate more effectively and lovingly about your feelings and needs.

Best used for: To aid difficult conversations between couples or family members.

How to use it: Pick a problem you want to talk about.

Look at the list of needs. Which of those needs aren't being met? Circle them.

Now look at the list of feelings. When those needs aren't met, which of these feelings do you have?

Share what you've found with a partner. Ask them to look at the same lists and identify what needs and feelings aren't being met for them.

Type of tool: Knowing/Reality transforming

64 From the Center for Nonviolent Communication https://www.cnvc.org/store/feelings-and-needs-inventory

Tool: Ho'oponopono Hawaiian Forgiveness Prayer[65]

Purpose: Healing other people or the separation between yourself and other people.

Best used for: Problems with people.

How to use it: Whenever a place for healing presents itself in your life, open to the place where the hurt resides within you. After identifying this place, with as much feeling as you can, say the below four statements:

I'm sorry
Please forgive me
Thank you
I love you

In doing this simple, powerful practice, it doesn't seem to matter whether I'm saying these words to myself, to my family, to God or to life itself. Just say them (or listen to them, there are a million videos to find and enjoy) and let them flow over you whenever you are afraid of your death or the death of someone else.

Type of tool: Knowing/Reality transforming

65 My favorite Ho'oponopono video where you repeat the prayer 108 times (a sacred number in Hinduism and Buddhism) Search YouTube for "Sandra Rolus Ho'oponopono 108 Repetitions".

About the Author

REV. SARA STEVENS NICHOLS is a spiritual leader, teacher, host of the "Conscious Reality Show" YouTube webcast, and public interest advocate. Her experience as a lawyer in Washington, D.C., the California legislature, and minister at the Center for Spiritual Awareness in West Sacramento bridges her work with a completely new reality. She has studied, practiced, and taught multiple tools including Science of Mind, Byron Katie's "The Work," the 12-Steps, Mary Morrissey's work, and the dynamic laws of Catherine Ponder. Sara is a fifth-generation Californian raised in San Diego with a legacy of authorship. Her grandmother, Sallie Stevens Nichols, wrote *Jung and Tarot: An Archetypal Journey* and her father, Prescott Stevens Nichols, was the author of multiple plays.

Sara lives with her husband, environmental leader Bill Magavern in an intentional community in downtown Sacramento. They have two adult children. To learn more about Sara, please visit:

www.sarastevensnichols.com

www.ingramcontent.com/pod-product-compliance
Lightning Source LLC
Jackson TN
JSHW030046130526
102270JS00002B/3

* 9 7 8 0 8 7 5 1 6 9 7 5 0 *